AF224147

Getting Started With DSLR Photography

A Beginner's Guide to Capturing Beautiful Photos With Your Digital Camera

Kevin Jobson

© Copyright 2020 - All rights reserved.

The content contained within this book may not be reproduced, duplicated or transmitted without direct written permission from the author or the publisher.

Under no circumstances will any blame or legal responsibility be held against the publisher, or author, for any damages, reparation, or monetary loss due to the information contained within this book, either directly or indirectly.

Legal Notice:

This book is copyright protected. It is only for personal use. You cannot amend, distribute, sell, use, quote or paraphrase any part, or the content within this book, without the consent of the author or publisher.

Disclaimer Notice:

Please note the information contained within this document is for educational and entertainment purposes only. All effort has been executed to present accurate, up to date, reliable, complete information. No warranties of any kind are declared or implied. Readers acknowledge that the author is not engaged in the rendering of legal, financial, medical or professional advice. The content within this book has been derived from various sources. Please consult a licensed professional before attempting any techniques outlined in this book.

By reading this document, the reader agrees that under no circumstances is the author responsible for any losses, direct or indirect, that are incurred as a result of the use of the information contained within this document, including, but not limited to, errors, omissions, or inaccuracies.

Table of Contents

Introduction

Taking eye-catching images may seem exclusive for professional photographers who own tons of equipment and have mastered the art of photography. While this may be true in a sense, there is very little stopping you from capturing beautiful images yourself. You may be the designated casual photographer at family gatherings, or maybe you want to dip your hands into the creative world of imagery. Either way, this book is where you begin—preparing you to start your journey into photography, earning money for your craft, or perfecting the task of capturing stunning memories for your family to cherish. Photography is an engaging discipline that draws the viewer into the moment— captured at the perfect time, the perfect angle, with the perfect lighting. It allows a person to enter into a past moment in time and feel what was felt or see what was seen. Photography is essentially a window to the past capturing beauty in a flash and preserving it for future generations to glimpse a piece of days past.

Photography is becoming increasingly available for almost anyone with a phone to create stunning visuals. However, phone photography has its limitations. Entering into digital DSLR photography will allow you greater opportunities to get creative, curate elegant scenes, and print images in bigger sizes. Owning a DSLR camera will give you the chance to manipulate light and turn it into magical scenes. With various settings and functions, having this type of camera and a bit of post-shoot editing skills gives you the ability to capture moments that are almost identical to what you see with your naked eye. Phone photography may be a great place to start, and with the phone cameras and functionality upgrading so often, you will be able to take stunning visuals. Yet having a camera will elevate those visuals to even greater heights, and the camera will always be able to do more than a phone can.

Another benefit of a DSLR camera is the variety of lenses and the ability to alternate between them. This means that you can select equipment that will aid you in whichever photography discipline that you feel drawn to. Zoom lenses help with wedding photography and wildlife. While certain lenses are good for portraiture, others are good for landscape visuals. In addition, you also have the ability to add more equipment to your camera bag, such as an external flash or a tripod. These can elevate your images to product photography standards and even magazine quality.

If you are inspired to move beyond photography and incorporate videography to your bag of tricks and skills, then a DSLR camera is again the necessary tool for your journey. Most cameras in this range offer video functionality. This allows you to intensify your skills and create a remarkable video without buying a video camera, which limits you by the inability to take photos. Investing in a DSLR gives you the power to dip your feet in both disciplines without compromising quality. Top of the range DSLR cameras are sometimes used in professional music videos in the place of specialized video cameras. This gives you the benefit of using one camera for two jobs if you are required to take stills and video for any project. Or even if you just want to capture some home videos along with your photos.

No matter what your motivation is to move on up to DSLR photography, you are making a great choice. The field may be an expensive one, but the rewards are worth it. Imagine hanging up the large canvas filled with the emotion of the family picnic; the smiling faces and laughter radiating out of the canvas and filling the room with love and warmth. Maybe you want that cold icy scene of your trip to the snow plastered above the fireplace to create an aesthetically pleasing contrast. Possibly you are wanting to start your journey to making a career out of photography and you are confused as to where to start, you have already learned that you can take impressive imagery using only your phone, but you wish you could light up a few more areas of the photograph or slow down the shutter to create a blur of motion to bring life to your scene. This book is here to give you the tools to set you up to understand why a DSLR camera offers so much more to your already creative skillset. It will guide you in purchasing the right camera for your budget, intentions, and goals. Then it will teach you the basics of all the settings on your camera to allow you to start learning the rules in order to break them in all the right places later on. The book will also help to inspire that creative spark inside of you and give you the ideas to begin your photographic creations of brilliance.

Throughout this book, there will be photography prompts to help motivate and inspire you to take outstanding photographs. At the bottom of select pages will be a photo challenge you can do as you read through the book or wait until the end and attempt the challenge once you are equipped with all the skills. If you don't have your camera yet, try them out using your phone, but be sure to go back and try them again once you have your camera and compare the difference. The prompts will be inspiring to enhance creativity, or they will be testing some of the knowledge that this book will impart based on the settings and functionality of the camera. Playing with light, or shutter speeds to manipulate the scenes in front of you to create something unique and which speaks to your inner creative. Let's get ready to aim, and let's get shooting!

Common Photography Terms

Aperture - This indicates how wide or how narrow the lens is opened to allow light in

Composition - The layout of the image which is made-up using framing and the elements in the image

DSLR - Digital Single Lens Reflex. This is a type of digital camera

Exposure - This is a measure of how light or dark your image comes out

Filter - A cover over the lens or editing tool which places a layer over the image to produce various effects

ISO - A unit to measure exposure. Depending on the sensor's sensitivity to light

JPEG - The most common format of images when saved on a computer

Lens - The attachment on the camera which filters the light through to the sensor. It also controls the aperture, and there are various focal lengths. There are different lenses with different capabilities

Pixel - A unit of measurement. Used to measure the information contained in an image

RAW - A format of images produced by professional digital cameras that are not yet processed

Shutter - The mirror flap inside the camera which flips open when an image is taken

Shoot, Shot, Shooting - Photography jargon, which refers to images. A shot is when you have taken an image by clicking the shutter while shooting means that you are busy taking many shots and a shoot is when you take a series of shots for a particular purpose

Viewfinder - The lens through which you look to see what the camera will capture when you take a shot

Digital Photography and DSLR

Digital photography is in close reach to so many people in the digital landscape that we are currently in. Specialized equipment for certain disciplines, such as photography, used to be limited to the wealthy because of the high prices, yet it has become more accessible and affordable in recent times. You only need a decent cellphone to take attractive images to upload on social media or send them to friends and family.

Even though it is rather easy to snap a quick photo of something with your device, it is not so easy to take professional-looking photos without knowing something about photography. The first step to understanding cameras is to know how they came about and what exactly sets them apart from cameras on other devices such as phones or laptops.

Not all digital photography is equal. As with any technology, photography equipment has evolved since the first digital cameras were created. Cameras are now offered for many different experience levels: entry-level cameras to top-range DSLR cameras. It's important to understand the differences to choose what is best suited for you.

Digital Photography

Kodak created the first digital camera in the 1970s. While it was highly advanced for the time, it was made using scraps and took over 20 seconds to capture a black and white image (Skipworth, 2014). Cameras have evolved over the years, and from the 1990s, consumer-friendly cameras were made available (Skipworth, 2014).

Now, with the evolution of cameras, it becomes increasingly difficult to know what to buy for your needs if you don't know too much about photography and cameras. You may be distrusting of salespeople and not know where to turn for advice. The absolute best way to go shopping for anything is to go armed with basic knowledge of the product, its history, and its competition. This book isn't a history lesson, though, so let's keep this brief.

Film vs Digital

Before the digital camera, the history of cameras went through many developments, the results of which were often big bulky cameras that took very long to produce images. The *camera obscura,* which was a large dark room with a pinhole that would let the light in from the objects outside, causing an inverted image to appear on the opposite white wall (The Editors of Encyclopedia Britannica, 2013), progressed to the film camera and finally, the digital cameras which we are so comfortable with today.

Film cameras were developed in the 1880s, with the Kodak camera being the first one (Ma, 2017). The film cameras built for consumers were popular as they were fairly simple and affordable. The simplicity of the camera allowed many consumers to handle them without needing to learn too much. The camera would allow light to enter once the shutter button had been pressed, and the light would imprint a reversed image onto the film, which was sitting inside the camera. The imprint was possible because the film used in the camera has strips of a silver halide solution covered by a layer of gelatin, which light would burn images onto (Hull, 2011).

The rolls of film used would allow the user to take multiple images before the roll was finished and needed to be removed to have the images developed. The development of images needs to be done in darkness, or else any unwanted light will ruin the film strips. Once the film has been removed from the camera and developed onto reels using developing tanks and chemical solutions in complete darkness, a red light can be used, allowing developers to create photographs from the developed film. The development process starts by dipping the film into chemicals that remove the coating and produce an inverse of the original image (Hull, 2011), to show the scene in the way the eyes perceived it.

In this process, the image could be projected from light machines to enlarge the image onto a large sheet of paper, so the end result would not be tiny images on small blocks of film.

Digital then came about and introduced a new way of capturing images. Instead of letting light in a hole to imprint on a piece of film inside the camera, digital became slightly more complicated. The digital cameras we see today have a sensor which is hypersensitive to light, and once the light coming in from the open shutter hits the sensor, it splits into small 'pieces' or digital waves which are stored as numbers to indicate the various brightness and colors of the 'pieces' known as pixels (Woodford, 2018). Now that the image you have taken is stored as numbers, it can be read and manipulated by other technology, such as computers.

Disadvantages of Digital

Digital photography does have its shortfalls, and some people still prefer to use film cameras. While it is most likely for nostalgic reasons, there are occasions where users feel more in-control with film cameras. This is because film cameras require the user to set all the settings themselves instead of using automatic functions. This enables the user to learn how to manipulate light to create unique and stunning visuals.

Digital camera users may rely on the automatic functions too heavily, causing the images to come out the same as everyone else's. Having a camera that allows you to be in control of all the light and aperture settings, but only using the automation functions, will result in dull images that may not always depict the scene that your eye is seeing. This is one way digital cameras can hinder your creative abilities and prevent you from taking your skills to the next level.

Digital cameras allow for easy snapping of images, and if you have a reasonably sized memory card, you can snap hundreds of images in one session. This can be a benefit if you are required to produce plenty of images in one go, but can also be a big disadvantage. Film cameras would only have a small roll of film which could produce 12, 24, or 36 images at a time. This meant that you needed to change the film more frequently. Most importantly, it meant that you would be forced to carefully think about your image, the composure, the lighting, etc. to not waste your film. Having a digital camera means that you can snap away and easily delete the less appealing images. This can cause you to be less mindful of setting up your image just right and relying more on producing a few appealing images if you take enough shots. With less thought going into each image, this can also lead to a lack of creativity and effort, which will prevent you from taking your images to a higher level.

Another issue is the cost of digital. Using a digital camera can become pricey if you are aiming for a more professional stance. The equipment and post-shoot software can start adding up to some hefty prices, and the cost to fix any broken equipment can also be quite high.

Advantages of Digital

Going digital obviously has its benefits. Apart from the convenience of being able to capture moments fairly easily and process them yourself if you have access to a computer and basic software, there are other benefits too.

Digital allows for more control. Just like the film camera required you to change all the settings yourself, digital cameras can be set to manual if you want to be in charge. With more options for settings to change, you can manipulate images far greater than you could with film cameras.

Having a digital camera allows you to capture and send images very quickly. Instead of needing to go to a photographic store to have your film developed, you can easily get the images yourself on your laptop or desktop computer.

Using digital imagery, you can go even further in your photo manipulation if you use photo editing software. With digital cameras capturing the light and immediately transferring them into a numbered sequence means that manipulation of the image is far greater than the limited tools you had to change film photographs.

Images taken with a digital camera can also be seen as the image is taken, and so any mistakes in the image can be rectified and the incorrect images deleted, straight away. Imagine waiting a whole week to have photos developed only to find out that your finger had been partially covering the top of the scene in every photograph.

Digital Single-Lens Reflex Cameras

Digital Single-Lens Reflex (DSLR) cameras are the cameras that are most commonly used in professional photography. Unless you are dealing with a creative photographer who uses various mediums such as film to create artistic creations, your average photographers will be using some type of DSLR camera.

What is a DSLR Camera and How Does It Work?

All cameras, including film cameras, used a single-lens reflex, which means that the light enters into the camera and imprints onto a piece of material. The analog version would open the shutter allowing the light to stream onto the film before closing again. The viewer would see the scene through a separate viewfinder, which would be slightly off what the image would depict, as the viewfinder did not look directly through the shutter.

With DSLR cameras, the light enters through the open shutter and hits a mirror or prism, which reflects the light up into the viewfinder. The user can now see exactly what the camera will capture as it is showing the scene through the shutter itself. Since the camera sensors actually depict the scene upside down, the mirror reflects it so that it is viewed the correct way up. Once the shutter button is pressed, the mirror snaps up to allow the light to reach the sensor which sits behind it (Bradford, 2019).

Point & Shoot Cameras

Point & shoot cameras are true to their name, in that you just have to point at your subject and snap a shot. This means that the settings are all automated, and the camera gauges the best settings to create sharp images. The problem with this is you are smarter than the camera, and your ability to play with settings will create more attractive shots than automated settings. Point & shoot cameras are mirrorless and do not have the most accurate view of the scene if you look through the viewfinder, as it is not showing you the picture through the actual lens. These cameras also show you the image on the screen as to how it will look once the image is taken, already putting the settings in practice. In contrast, looking through the viewfinder of DSLR cameras will show you the scene exactly as it is and not how it will look after taking a picture with your current settings. For instance, you may have a well-lit scene in front of you, which comes out too dark once you snap away with your DSLR camera if your settings are causing the image to be underexposed.

Point & shoot cameras are well-suited for those holiday pictures as they easily fit into your bag and are not too expensive to worry about while on a trip. Yet, if you want to capture those beautifully happy moments at a wedding for the bride and groom, then a DSLR is a must.

Why DSLR and Not Point & Shoot

DSLR cameras are the preferred choice over point and shoot because the photographer can control the outcome of the image. Whether the desire is to take sharp images of emotional moments, freeze them in time, or to create artistic images with motion-blur, the artist is in control. The functionality of DSLR cameras is versatile and enables the user to set up the image as they need to. Using additional equipment, time-lapse photos can be taken to track stars in the night sky, or long-exposure to light up a dark nighttime scene. Alternatively, the user can play with the aperture and shutter speeds to blur out parts of the image and create depth-of-field. These capabilities are not possible using a point & shoot camera, as the camera decides what the acceptable settings are, and that is it. If these settings aren't correctly manipulated while taking the image, it may not be salvageable in post-shoot editing. Without the correct exposure, the information in the image can be lost, and even the best Photoshop skills cannot create something that isn't there. Thus, if you are looking at photography to become a professional journey or a hobby which you want to see where it leads, then a DSLR camera is the better choice to tap into your creative genius and create attractive photographs.

Formatting: JPEG vs. RAW

You may already know and understand the JPEG format as most images you have dealt with have probably been in JPEG format. RAW may be a new term to you, and once you begin your photographic journey using a DSLR camera, you should become accustomed to this format, especially if you intend on using software to conduct post-shoot editing.

JPEG

JPEG or JPG is one of the standard formats of digital images. There are multiple others, such as PNG, TIFF, GIF, and so on. JPEG stands for "Joint Photographic Experts Group." This long name doesn't mean too much, as even those not interested in photography at all can understand and use JPEG images. The JPEG format compresses the image to create a compact file size, which reduces the amount of space that it will take up on your device. The problem with JPEG is that it reduces the quality of the image to a certain degree, and if you want to edit the image using software, you will reduce the quality even more if you are editing a JPEG file. This format is mainly used for the final product, to compact it to accessible and relatively small file sizes.

RAW

RAW is a less known unprocessed image format that is used by professional photographers. When shooting with a high-end camera, you can set the camera to generate images in RAW format. Some cameras allow a dual save in which you can generate the image twice, in JPEG and RAW format. RAW is what its name implies; these images are unprocessed or minimally processed by the camera. It will show the raw data that your camera has produced, whereas the JPEG version will be slightly processed with regards to the lighting and the sharpness of the image.

Photographers tend to use the RAW format as this is the best file to use in editing software. Since the image is unprocessed, any processing you do to it will impact the quality less than a JPEG formatted image. The issue with the RAW format is that not every computer can view these files without having higher-end software such as Adobe Photoshop or Lightroom. If you open the RAW image in a program such as Photoshop, you will be able to do an initial but limited edit, that will not affect the quality of the image in any way. These edits include changing the exposure, contrast, cropping, light balance, and saturation. This is highly beneficial if you would like to lightly correct any mistakes in the image without damaging the code of the image.

Once you begin to edit an image past this stage, you will be affecting the quality to some degree. This is not to worry as good cameras can produce hardy images that can withstand editing while still keeping the quality high.

Buying Tips for DSLR Cameras

All that information may have left your head spinning slightly, and now you are more confused about what camera to look at buying. Don't panic; these tips will be sure to aid you in making your decision on which camera to buy for your specific needs.

Firstly, decide if DSLR is the right category for you. If you are looking for a light-weight camera to carry in your backpack on your annual holiday without stressing about expensive equipment, then maybe a point & shoot is more suitable. If that is the case, don't put away this book just yet. Even if you are not interested in a DSLR camera, you will still be sure to find some tips and tricks to get your holiday pictures to the next level.

Once you have decided to get a DSLR camera as you want to be more professional, you need to decide on the brand you like. The two leading brands are Canon and Nikon, yet Sony is making its way up there very quickly. If you have met a photographer, you will surely know about the great Canon vs. Nikon rivalry. Every Canon owner will insist that you go for a Canon device while every Nikon owner will say the same about Nikon. The truth is you cannot go wrong with either brand. The important part is to decide on your experience level.

Cameras are divided into various ranges, starting from entry-level cameras to high-end professional cameras. A big difference that affects price within these ranges is whether the camera is a full frame or crop frame; an indicator of the size and quality of the camera's sensor. Full frame cameras are similar to the film camera due to their sensor size being equivalent to the 35mm film that the images were produced on. Crop frame cameras have a physically smaller sensor size in addition to capturing a cropped frame of view. Full frame cameras produce better quality images than the crop frame, and the consequence is that they cost more to manufacture and are quite expensive to buy. If you are shooting professionally or considering architectural photography, a full frame is a good option to go for. Crop frame cameras are better suited for beginners and photographers who use telephoto lenses for wildlife or sports, as it gives a slightly longer focal length as a result of the cropped frame. Most importantly, the low prices make it affordable for those getting started with photography.

Since you are only starting out, the high-end cameras are not necessary at this point. Although, you should do additional research into which entry-level camera will best suit your needs. Most people starting out in DSLR photography will look at the entry-level cameras as a starting point.

There is absolutely nothing wrong with purchasing a cheaper model at the beginning; it is safer in case you learn that photography just isn't for you, and second-hand cameras can sell really well if you have looked after it.

Second-hand cameras are a good option for beginners too, as long as it was well-looked after there shouldn't be many issues. Due to this being quite an expensive hobby generally, you can save some money going this route at the beginning.

Be sure to look at a camera with changeable lenses as this will allow you to expand your lens collection later on as you find your style of photography and your preferred subjects in front of the lens. A prime lens is usually a fixed lens that does not have a zoom function and comes standard with a number of camera bodies. This is a great lens to get started with.

If your budget is tight, you can choose to buy a camera body on its own and purchase the relatively affordable prime lens, known as the "nifty fifty." It may be less versatile as it has a fixed focal length meaning you cannot be too close to your subjects when taking the image, but it is a great lens to have. Alternatively, you can look at other affordable lenses and go with one of those as your first lens. Remember, lenses are something that you can always expand on later in your journey.

Most importantly, do your research! Before buying something as expensive as a DSLR camera, you should have an idea of what you want before you go into the shop. Salespeople can often be pushy and steer you towards a more expensive option by using fancy words and persuading you that it is the camera you need. Have a list of entry-level cameras in mind and check the prices online so that when you do go in, you can tell them your budget and insist that they cannot sell anything above that price. Knowledge is really powerful, and it will save you some money for some cool lenses or other equipment later on.

Shooting Prompt: Go out and take a photograph that will look good in black and white. Edit it using free or paid software and see how it comes out. High contrast images work well for black and white photography. Try setting your camera to take both RAW and JPEG and use the B&W setting if your camera has one.

Looking at Lenses

When you are purchasing your camera, you may notice that there are so many different lenses to choose from. All the different lengths and shapes, some fatter, and others slim, can be confusing, to say the least. If you are only a beginner and still testing the waters, you will be okay using just one lens for your learning. If you know that photography is what you want to do and you have your eyes set on buying various lenses, then you can still phase them in and buy them slowly to build up your collection. Good quality lenses can become very expensive, and each lens serves a different purpose. So whatever your skill level in taking photos is and where you want to go with your photo taking, it is important to know what situation each lens is suited for.

How Do Lenses Work With Your DSLR?

The majority of DSLR cameras have the option to change the lens on the camera. Some cameras are even sold separately just as a body without any lens, leaving it to the user to decide which lens to purchase.

Each lens will offer a different function and serve a different purpose; it is not as simple as buying any lens and fitting it on. Each brand of camera has its own mounting system for lenses, so if you are trying to borrow a lens from a friend with a different make or model camera, it may not fit on your camera. Thus, it is important to research and make sure that the lens you have chosen to buy will fit on your camera. Most brands will sell lenses that fit most of their models, but if you are on a tighter budget, you can also look at generic lenses that are cheaper and can fit on your camera despite being a different brand.

Some nostalgic photographers still use lenses designed for film cameras as the mount has been continued through the brand. Once the lens has been fitted onto your camera, you can now shoot photographs with the capabilities that the lens allows. These can be zoom functions or aperture functions. It is important to note that when you are changing a lens, you are opening up the camera and its sensitive sensor to the elements. Since it is a fixed sensor that lives in the camera, you should be sure to look after it to keep taking quality photographs. Once the camera is open, dust can fall in and harm the sensor, so tilt the camera downwards when changing lenses to take care of that sensor.

The Importance of Alternating Lenses

When buying a lens, you will notice that it is labeled with some information, the two most important being a length in millimeters (mm) and a number preceded by an f, which is known as an f-stop.

Firstly, the mm number is the focal length. This is the distance that the end of the lens can be from the camera's sensor. For instance, if you purchase a 16-35mm lens, this means that you can change the distance of your lens to some degree, meaning that it has a zoom function. If the lens says a fixed number such as a 50mm lens, this means that it is a fixed focal length, and you cannot zoom at all. It is important to know how much movement you would like your lens to be capable of. If you are shooting wildlife or moving objects, you may want a bit of zoom to be able to follow the subjects when they move closer or further away from you.

The second important detail is the f-number. This refers to the camera's f-stop, which is the amount the aperture can be manipulated. f-stops will affect your images, and you can use them to create different effects in your images. This will be explained in the aperture section of the book in chapter 5.

If you want to create unique and stunning visuals, you will need to alternate lenses for the various subjects you are shooting. It does not mean that you need to have one of every type of lens but you should have a few that suit your subjects and photography style if you want to take photography seriously.

Lenses and When to Use Them

The type of lens you buy and the focal length and aperture will all play a part in which lens you will use at any given time. It is important to use the right lens for a situation if you would like to get the best results out of your photography.

If you are taking photographs at a wedding, you will want to have a good zoom lens which is not too bulky or heavy to carry around, to take some inconspicuous shots. Moving away from the action lets you capture those emotional moments, without the subjects feeling self-conscious of having a camera pointed at them. Most wedding photographers will actually carry two cameras to have two lens setups, which they can quickly alternate between to be sure to capture each moment as it happens, both close to them and far away.

If your interest is wildlife, then an even stronger zoom lens is necessary. You will most likely be taking images of subjects that are far away. Your lens could also have an anti-glare cover which will prevent lens flare from the sun. This setup will most likely use a tripod or some sort of stabilizer to make sure the heavy lens can be held steady while shooting.

Lenses can become complicated, but a good rule of thumb to follow is if you are not using a tripod, then whatever mm you are shooting at, your shutter speed should be slightly higher to take sharp images that keep your subjects in focus. Using this method will ensure that you avoid camera shake, which will lead to blurry images. So if you are shooting with a 50mm lens, don't reduce your shutter speed to below $1/50^{th}$ of a second, unless you are using a stabilizer such as a tripod.

Wide-angle Lens

Wide-angle lenses are what their name describes; they are able to see past the scope of the human eye. The focal length can indicate which lenses are wide-angle: the smaller the focal length, the wider the angle. Anything below a 35mm lens is considered a wide-angle. If the focal length gets too low, then it becomes a fish-eye lens. The wide-angle lenses can be fixed length, or they can have the ability to zoom.

The purpose of a wide-angle lens is to give the photograph some depth and create a sense of inclusion. The key feature of this lens is that it causes the objects that are close to look slightly larger than the ones that are further away. The images tend to have a slight curve to them, which draws the viewer in.

These lenses are well suited for landscape photography to include more into the image or architecture photography, and especially in interior photography. The angle allows you to incorporate more into the image without needing to step back, which is advantageous if you are in a very tight space.

Fish-eye Lens

The lenses with extremely low focal lengths are known as fish-eye lenses. This type of lens allows for even more of the scene to be included in the image, but to fit more in the frame, the image becomes rounded and can capture a 180-degree view. GoPro cameras have a built-in fish-eye lens, giving that signature round shape to the images. The rounding of the image is known as lens distortion, which can be corrected in Photoshop if shooting in RAW. While there is the ability to straighten these images to a certain degree, the main point of using this lens would be to create that rounded effect for creative reasons.

This lens gives the photographer the ability to create unique and creative scenes. An example is to capture the subject close up to the camera while the background becomes smaller to pronounce the subject of the image.

These lenses can be used in the same way as wide-angle lenses, but they are suited more for creative use. Just because you can fit more into an image, doesn't mean that you always should. These lenses are often used to photograph action sport or cityscapes.

Zoom Lens

Zoom lenses are the lenses with which you can easily change the focal length without putting on a new lens. This allows you to have a flexible focal length. Zoom lenses make it convenient when you need to change the length of your shot quickly, without having to physically move around. The numbers on these lenses indicate the shortest and longest focal length that the camera can adjust to. A 16-35mm lens will allow you to zoom anywhere between those two focal lengths by twisting the adjustable ring of the lens. The aperture on these lenses varies from fixed to an aperture range. The focal length will usually affect the aperture limits.

The purpose of these lenses is to allow you to quickly adjust if you need to get a close up of something far away as well as shots of the subjects that are closer to you. This helps with objects that are constantly moving or if you want to get different perspectives of the landscape in front of you.

Wedding photographers may utilize them on one camera with a telephoto lens on the other. Portraits can also be taken with a zoom lens because of the sharpness which the lens provides. Zoom lenses can also be used in everyday scenarios as they allow for a fairly versatile range of capabilities.

Telephoto Lens

A telephoto lens allows for an even greater 'zoom' for your camera. While these lenses capture subjects at great distances, they are not all zoom lenses, and some may have a fixed focal length. What makes it a telephoto lens is if the focal length is higher than 60mm. These lenses can become quite big and bulky if you go for a very high focal length.

These lenses are great for getting up close to objects that are far away and not so clear to the average eye. They tend to magnify the scene so that you feel up close to the subject in the distance.

Telephoto lenses are mainly used in wildlife photography or in sports photography. They can also be used in wedding photography, and some portrait photographers may use them for their focus and their ability to blur out the background of an image. Tripods are often used to stabilize these lenses because of their weight.

Macro Lens

A macro lens is the opposite of the telephoto lens and allows the photographer to get up close and personal with very small objects. You may have tried to focus your phone camera before and realized that the camera could not focus on the subject as the camera is too close to it. The macro lens will allow you to get even closer while still producing a sharp image. The focal length of these cameras can vary between 40 to 200mm. You would need to make sure that the lens is called a macro lens before purchasing based on a focal length.

These lenses are used to capture subjects that are extremely close up, keeping that image incredibly sharp. They are sometimes used in portrait photography, too, for that signature sharpness that they offer.

The "Nifty Fifty" 50mm Lens

The 50mm lens is often praised by some photographers as being a perfect lens to start off with. This lens is fixed at a focal length of 50mm and offers a wide aperture catering for images with a shallow depth of field. This wide opening of the aperture, which is a key feature of this lens allows the user to heavily blur out the background while keeping the subject in sharp focus. Even though the focal length cannot be changed, this lens is incredibly versatile.

The use of this lens is to focus the image on one subject by blurring out the unnecessary bits. At the same time, it can also offer clear landscape images with everything in focus when the aperture is narrowed.

From portraits to landscapes to street photography, this lens is one of the most versatile you can get. Another upside of this lens is the price, as they are relatively inexpensive throughout the various brands.

Tips for Buying Lenses

Buying a new lens is a big step, and the decision on which lens to buy should be carefully thought out. Lenses can be very pricey, and if they are not suited for your interests, you will not get your money's worth. You can use the above as a guide to which type of lens you will need, then research the best lenses in those categories. Do not rush into buying fancy lenses straight away if you think that will help you take great shots. Master your prime lens first. Play around with the functions until you understand the camera settings and how everything works. Once you have begun taking well-balanced, appealing photographs, then move on to a new lens.

Be wary of cheap lenses. While your budget may be tight, you could be enticed to go for a lens that has a very small price tag. But, when it comes to camera lenses, you really do get what you pay for. So if you can, look at the high-end lenses if you truly want your images to look sharp and professional.

Research the type of functions you want to be able to do with your new lens and have a look at which lenses will give you that functionality. If you are unsure if a lens will give you the capabilities you are looking for, but you would still like to try out the lens, then look at buying a second-hand lens. It is not a bad thing to buy second-hand, but check that the equipment was well looked after.

Be sure to check the aperture which you are needing, and decide what focal length you will most likely be using. Lenses that "do it all" are not necessarily the best buy because if you want to specialize in a certain avenue of photography, then you do require a specialized lens.

Remember to take the weight and size of the lens into consideration. If you want to take your camera hiking to capture some nature scenes, then a big heavy telephoto lens is probably not the best choice. If you want to take sports photographs and you need a bulky lens, be sure that you have a tripod to stabilize the lens, or a monopod would also work well.

Shooting Prompt: If your lens has an adjustable focal point, take the image using the lowest and then the highest length and see the different compositions which it produces. You will notice how the perspective changes.

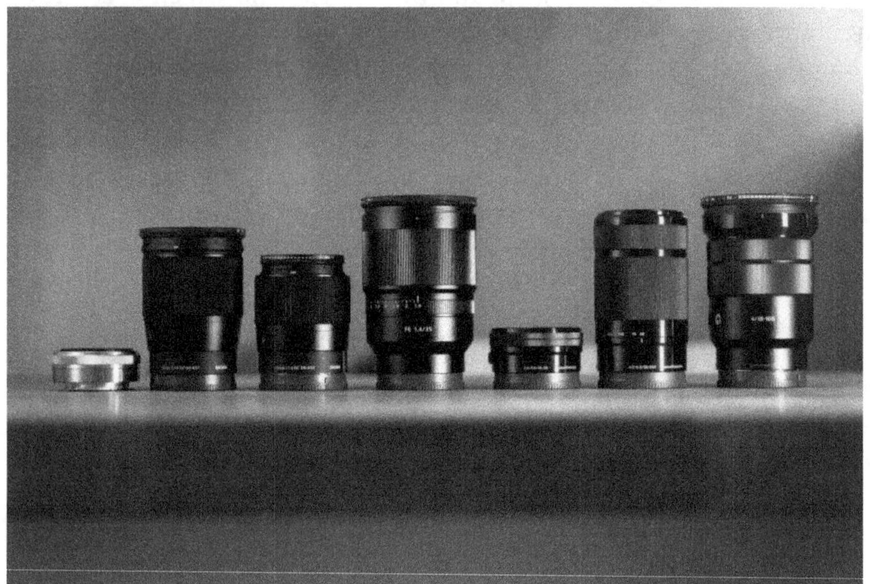

Filters

You may be familiar with the term filters from social media: the
Snapchat and Instagram images with colors over them or sparkling
stars and dog ears. While these could be seen as having been inspired
by camera filters, they work slightly differently. Photography filters are
fairly inexpensive covers that attach to the front of your lens. The filter
is a round ring with glass or resin in the center with different properties
depending on the type of filter you buy.

Why Are Filters Used in Photography?

Filters are used in photography for two main reasons. Firstly, the filter
alters the image in certain ways in order to produce the desired effects
on the image. This is done by altering the light as it passes through the
filter that may or may not have a colored tint to it. Secondly, a filter
acts as a great lens protector by stopping any dust or dirt from affecting
the lens as well as to prevent scratches or cracks on the actual lens, as
the glass of a filter is more durable than the glass on the lens. Plus, it is
much easier and safer to clean the filter than your lens if there are any
smudge marks or fingerprints. Filters have slightly lost their popularity
due to the ability to add filters over the image in post-processing.
However, there are always limits to your editing before it becomes
destructive. Filters are good options to have because of their low price
and because it is so much easier to replace a filter than a whole lens.

Types of Filters

Filters vary widely for their variety of different uses. You can pick up
fairly cheap UV filters if you are only looking to protect your lens, or

you can find a specialized filter if you are looking to produce a unique effect.

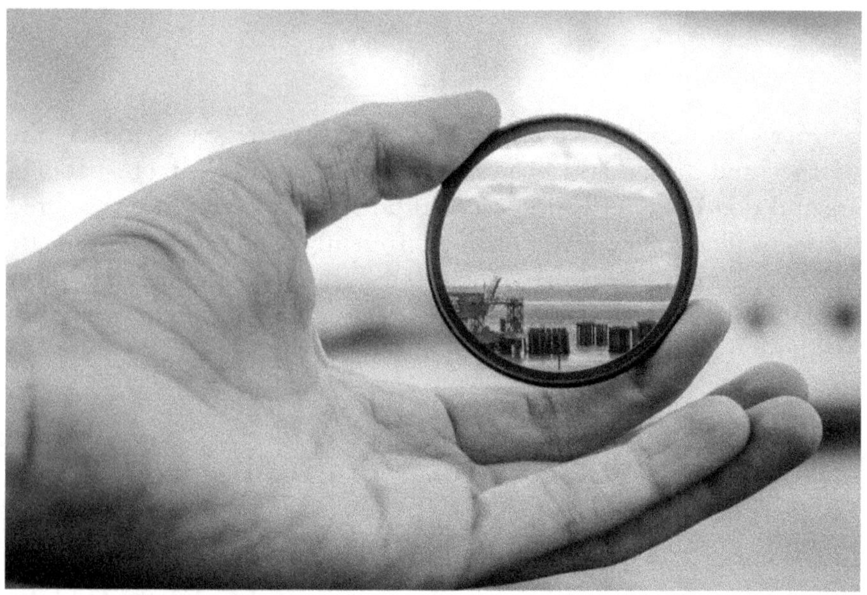

Polarizing Filter

These filters are used to create a polarizing effect on your image. The filter does this by blocking reflected light or glare from entering your lens, resulting in a clearer image with stronger colors. If you are shooting objects with reflective surfaces such as bodies of water, you will be able to enhance the image by bringing out the water and what is below it instead of bringing out the reflections (Ives, 2015). This filter will definitely not be useful if you are trying to get those reflections in the water to pop out.

This filter is best used for outdoor scenes to bring out the vibrant colors and cut through transparent reflective surfaces. It would be hard to achieve a true polarizing effect in post-shoot editing as the information for what is below the water or object will not have transferred to the camera. It is, however, possible to make the colors pop more in editing, but the effects won't be as natural as they would be if you used the filter.

UV Filters

UV filters are the best-suited filter for lens protection. These filters were necessary for the era of the film as they would prevent too much UV light from hitting the sensitive film, which resulted in unwanted blue tints (Ives, 2015). The sensors in the digital cameras are not sensitive to UV light, and so there is not much need for UV filters for the actual image. Yet, they are still very useful for that protection, and they are small, light, and affordable. Be sure to take note of buying ones which are extremely cheap, because as with everything in photography you get what you pay for. Some lower range filters may produce a less sharp image, so it is worth the investment to look for a good quality filter.

Neutral Density Filters

Neutral density filters help to reduce the amount of light that enters your camera. This is very helpful when you are shooting on very bright days and would like to play with your camera settings more, without continuously fighting overexposure. As the neutral in the name implies, these filters do not alter the color of your image or affect it in any way in that regard. These filters are great if you would like to use slow shutter speeds in well-lit conditions. Using this filter, you can open up the shutter to create those glassy lake scenes you may be familiar with.

Graduated Neutral Density Filters

This type of filter is very similar to the neutral density filter. It also stops too much light from entering without changing the color of the light. The difference here is that it causes a gradient effect so that you can use it to prevent the sky from overexposure while still keeping the rest of the scene at the correct exposure. This results in only half of the image being corrected in terms of light. If you have ever tried to get the exposure right during sunrise, you will surely know of the battle to get the whole image correctly exposed. Either the light blows out the sky or the foreground scene comes out too dark. Post-shoot editing will have a hard time correcting this if too much information is lost due to over or underexposure. There are now options in Adobe products to apply a graduated neutral density filter over the image, but again, the image processing can reduce the quality.

Color Correcting Filters

These filters are the ones with a visible colored tint on the glass. It is important to understand how colors work with light in order to know which colored filter is suited for you, as these filters can be found in either cooling or warming colors. A warming filter will give the image a more intense orangey color, while the cooling filters offer a blue tint. These effects result in a warm image with an autumn-type feel or a gloomy blue-tinted image. This is not to say that your image will come out blue or orange; it will correct the color distortion and produce a more naturally lit image. You may have seen an inside shot taken at night when the orange glow of the lightbulb makes the whole scene come out too orange. Using a cooling filter will alter the orange light from the source to create a more neutral color. This can be used vice versa for when you need an image to be warmer.

Shooting Prompt: Hold a piece of colored transparent plastic over half of your lens. Make sure it is as clean and smooth as possible. See how it affects half of your image.

Additional Camera Equipment

Photographers are often characterized as people carrying large bags on their backs, struggling under long tripod bags draped over their shoulders, and a camera dangling from their necks. Then they go back to fetch a huge block bag with their prized telephoto lens. While some photographers choose to travel light with just a camera in their hand and the strap wrapped around their wrist, the amount of baggage you need depends on your area of expertise. For example, a tripod is a must for long exposure and heavy lenses, and some photographers would benefit from having a tripod to produce extra sharp images with their normal zoom lenses and average shutter speeds. Here are just a few bits of equipment that may aid you as you take your photography to the next level.

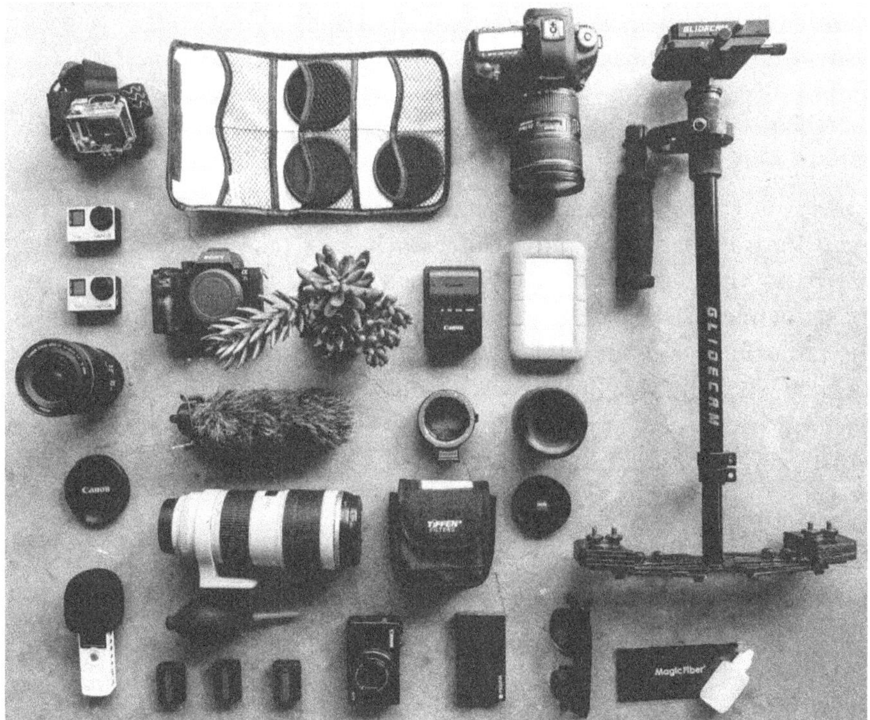

Stability Equipment

Tripod/Monopod

A tripod is a contraption with three legs, which helps to stabilize the camera. Once your camera is mounted on the tripod, you can change the level to straighten the camera. Some tripods offer various tilting options, allowing you to shoot both landscape and portrait. Some tripods can be very restrictive as your camera cannot move around so easily, so be sure to buy a tripod suited for your needs. These are best for long-exposure shots such as night-time photography and to create motion blur while keeping your camera stable.

A monopod is a long stick that mounts the camera on top. This is very useful if you need to stabilize your camera or are using a heavy lens but need to be very mobile and flexible. These are best suited for sport and wildlife photography, as well as action sports.

Remote Shutter Release

When using a tripod, it helps to have a remote shutter release. This is a wired button that plugs into your camera and takes the picture when you press the button. This is very useful if you need to take sharp images while using long-exposures. When using slow shutter speeds, the camera is very sensitive to movement, so even the small act of pressing the shutter button can cause camera shake and produce unsharp and blurry images. This way, you can step away from the camera and release the shutter without shaking the camera in any way.

Lens Extender

When using telephoto lenses, you may want to zoom in closer to objects, but your lens is at its fullest, and you cannot afford to buy a new lens, or you would just like more versatility with your lenses. A lens extender attaches to the camera before the lens is connected, and then the lens fits on top of the extender. This will magnify your zoom by the number on the extender. Be wary as the extenders do limit your aperture despite the capabilities of the lens. For example, the lens' maximum aperture will be decreased by a stop or two: a 1.4x extender reduces it by one stop, while a 2x extender decreases it by two stops. On the other hand, your 200mm lens will now have 400mm capabilities if you attach a 2x extender to your camera.

Light Equipment

External Flash

Most DSLR cameras come with a built-in flash, but professional photographers rarely use this flash. The problem with built-in flashes on cameras is its distance to the lens; having a light source close to the lens tends to blow out the image leading to overexposure. The subject is lit in a very harsh light, and the results are not very pleasing. External flashes mount on top of your camera and have a fairly long tube before the flash source, giving a more diffused light source.

The top half of the flash tube can be swiveled around to point upwards, straight ahead or to the sides, giving the photographer flexibility to bounce the light off reflectors. Photographers strategically point the flash towards the roof to create a diffused light by reflecting the harsh light off the ceiling or other colored objects. This diffused light gives subtler and natural lighting to the subjects. Most flashes also come with a small diffuser and reflector attached to the top, which can be flipped over the light source for a diffused effect.

Gray Card

A gray card is an effective and inexpensive way to manage your exposure levels in areas where you have a constant light source.

Sometimes cameras will incorrectly judge the exposure if it is trying to read a scene with multiple exposure ratings and usually when pure black or white objects are involved. This is because the camera meter is working to calculate an 18% gray when metering exposure (McIntire, 2016). Thus, your image may come out slightly off-color with an incorrect exposure. Putting the gray card in your shot to focus on when testing exposure will help correct the image. Set your camera to manual when adjusting this and auto white balance and then change your settings while focusing on the card. Then remove the card from your shot and snap away.

Reflectors

Reflectors are very handy in adjusting the light in various scenes. A reflector is a reflective surface that is used to bounce light off of. You can buy specialized ones or make your own by using a shiny white piece of cardboard. The reflector is used to control the lighting. It can be used to light certain parts of the image that are slightly underexposed or to fill in shadows that the main light source does not reach. The reflector must be aimed at an angle that allows the main light source to reach it and bounce it in the direction of the area you want to light up. It offers a soft diffused light so it can also be used to move the object away from harsh light sources, such as the sun, and light it up using the softer reflected light.

Lightbox

A lightbox is useful in creating studio setups. It creates a diffused light source that allows you to place objects in the center to light up the object with a complete light source coming from all angles. It takes away any shadows so the object is evenly lit. These will most likely be used in product photography, and you can quite easily make your own at home.

Accessibility

Spare Memory Cards

It is always a good idea to carry more than one memory card. With digital cameras giving you the ability to snap away without worrying about changing films, you must remember that memory cards also have their limits. If you do not clear your memory card regularly, you may be out on a project and realize that you have no more space, as taking videos always requires a lot of space.

Spare Batteries

Another one to remember is always to charge your batteries after each project. Even when they are not in use, the batteries could slowly lose power too. So it is crucial to have back-up batteries to be well-prepared. Imagine running out of power half-way through a wedding ceremony.

Cleaning Kit

It is important to have a decent cleaning kit for your camera. You may be tasked with shooting in dusty areas or on beaches and areas with lots of sand or dirt. You want to be sure to keep your camera as far from the elements as possible, but it is very easy to get dust on the lens and the body of the camera. Having a brush, blower, and cloth can help you look after your equipment when out shooting. Be sure not to meddle inside the camera as you can easily damage the sensor. If there are spots on your images and you can't fix it by cleaning the lens, it will be better to take your camera into a professional photography shop to have it cleaned inside.

Camera Strap

A camera strap is definitely necessary in order to keep your camera safe. Most photographers wear it around their necks, so if your camera does slip, it will not get damaged. Also, a strap is a great way to hold your camera when you need your hands free to fix up the scene.

Shooting Prompt: Take a portrait using window lighting. Place your subject next to the window and facing you, so their side is facing the window. See how the light lights up their one side. Next, hold a big reflective surface, such as a mirror or white cardboard up on their other side, so it reflects the window light, and you will notice the difference.

Exposure

Lighting and exposure are so important for photography. So far, you know that images are made up of light that imprints on some sort of sensor or film. So managing the light that enters the camera is extremely important in order to capture the image in a way that presents it how you want it to be represented. Letting too much light in will blow out the image and lose a lot of the detail, while letting in too little light will result in a dark image where you cannot see the subjects well enough.

What is Exposure?

Simply put, exposure is the amount of light that is let into the camera to allow the image to be imprinted on the film or the sensor. The light is let in when the shutter opens after the shutter release button is pressed. In DSLR cameras, this is the moment when the mirror is flipped to allow the light to reach the sensor.

Exposure can be managed in a few different ways. Outside of the camera, if you are using artificial light sources, you can alter the light to brighten up or darken your scene. Yet, in a lot of cases, you cannot control the light source, especially if that source is the sun. The camera gives you three main ways to alter the exposure levels: ISO, shutter speed, and aperture. The camera focuses on spots in the image, and if this isn't accurate for the entire image, some areas will not be correctly exposed.

The three settings together create an exposure value or EV. Some DSLR cameras will display the EV on the small screen on top of the camera while others have an EV or light meter in the viewfinder. This is shown by a line with the numbers -3, -2, -1, 0, 1, 2, 3. As you manipulate the three different settings, you will see a 'needle' somewhere along that line showing the photographer if the image is underexposed or overexposed. The prime exposure is when the needle is sitting on the 0. Between the numbers are two short lines, and each line and number on the light meter represents an f-stop. The below settings are all measured in f-stops, and adjusting them will see the meter shift to raise or lower the f-stop. Not every image should have an EV of 0, playing around by slightly over or underexposing the image can produce unique effects.

Overexposure

When too much light is let in, the result is an image that is blown out. The highlights of the image can become completely white, and what is in the scene will be lost. You can produce an image that is exposed correctly in some areas while others are overexposed, often seen when someone is trying to take images of a landscape with the sun included. The camera will focus on the sky or the land, causing the other area to be exposed incorrectly. When the camera measures exposure using the land in the foreground, the sky will most likely become overexposed if it is much brighter than the foreground.

Underexposure

Underexposure is the complete opposite. This occurs when there is not enough light let into the camera, causing parts of the image to be too dark and reaching complete black at points. Once you lose too much information when taking an image that is too dark, you won't be able to correct it in post-shoot editing. Using the above example, if you focused your exposure on the sun, you might lose areas of the foreground as they will be too dark. Using filters can assist in capturing correct exposure, as well as editing post-shoot with editing software. Although to be certain that you do not miss out on any details in your image, it is best if you use the camera settings to ensure that your image is exposed correctly.

ISO

ISO is one of the camera settings which you can use to ensure that you expose your image correctly. ISO stands for International Standards Organization, and is the rating of the sensor with regards to light sensitivity, meaning the strength of the sensor to pick up the light let into the camera. By increasing your ISO, you are programming the sensor to be more sensitive to light resulting in a brighter image. This means that you can lighten up darker scenes to a certain degree by adjusting your ISO.

This setting is the most fixed of the three relating to exposure and you shouldn't need to alter your ISO too much during a shoot. When arriving at the spot you are shooting at you should decide a base ISO which will work well with the available lighting. The other two settings are much easier to adjust during the session.

If you are shooting in well-lit conditions such as in bright sunlight, then your ISO should be fairly low, at about 100 to 200 is standard for sunlit scenes. This means that the sensor will not be extremely sensitive to light and therefore the sun will not burn out areas of your image and cause overexposure.

On the other side, if you are shooting darker scenes such as night-time scenes or indoor shots you will most likely need to raise your ISO up higher. There is a limit to how high you should set your ISO, even if the camera can go to a high ISO of about 6 400, it is not necessarily a good thing to set it this high.

The downside of using your ISO to control exposure is that if the sensor becomes too sensitive then it will create noise on your image, resulting in a grainy effect that you will see on the image. Some photographs are captured with an intentionally high ISO in order to create the grain effect in a creative situation. However, if the grainy texture of the image is not intended, then it is best to ensure that your ISO is low enough to not produce noise. The ISO limits will vary from camera to camera, but generally going above 1 200 ISO is pushing the limits, this is around the point where the image loses its sharpness to the noise. Some cameras can safely push it above that while creating sharp images but not all cameras will.

While you will adjust all three settings together to create the exact effects that you want, the ISO should be your base setting. In harsh sunlight, you should use an ISO of 100 to 200, in shady or cloudy conditions 200 to 400. If it is indoors use 400 to 800 ISO, while indoors at night should be around 800 to 1 200. Only in extreme low light conditions and if you don't mind getting a bit of noise in your image then bump it up to 3 200. Test your camera before shooting professionally in order to see how high you can push your camera's ISO before it becomes noisy and loses its sharpness.

Aperture

What is it?

The aperture refers to how wide open the shutter is. The wider you set your aperture, the more light that is able to enter the camera, allowing you to expose the scene in low light conditions. The aperture functions in two ways, the first being the amount of light that is let into the camera, and the second is the ability to add depth of field to the image. The depth of field is what makes the image look as though objects are nearer and further away from the camera. A shallow depth of field is when the subject of the image is in focus while the rest of the image is blurred out to some degree.

This shallow depth gives the viewer the ability to almost step into the image or feel as though they can reach in and take the object out of the image. A deep depth of field, on the other hand, is when the whole image is sharp and in focus. When setting the aperture, you need to take both the need for light and depth of field into consideration. The depth of field is important when thinking of how you want the image to turn out, as a well thought out balance will create an aesthetically pleasing photograph.

The numbers on the lens will give you an indication of the aperture settings that it is capable of achieving, represented by two numbers indicating the highest and lowest aperture setting available. These are known as f-stops, and some lenses come with a fixed aperture, which is indicated by one number. The f-stop can be represented as f2.8, f/2.8, or 1:2.8, with the most common being f2.8.

The aperture is wide when the f-stop number is low, meaning that a lens with an f-stop of f1.8 can open wider than one with f2.8 as the lowest aperture. These low numbers indicate that the image will have a shallow depth of field. The higher the number goes, the less light is let in, resulting in a deep depth of field, meaning that the image is, for the most part, sharp and in focus.

While keeping in mind the type of depth of field you want your image to have, you need to weigh it against the amount of light that you have let in. This must once again be weighed against the ISO you have set and the shutter speed you require to take a sharp photograph.

When to Adjust It

You should use a shallow depth of field when you want the image to focus on one object without a distracting background. This is used in portrait photography, macro photography, and sometimes in sports photography.

A deep depth of field is more suited for groups of people, landscapes, in order to get the whole scene sharp, and product photography.

Aperture is fun to play around with, get creative and see what magic you can create with your aperture setting.

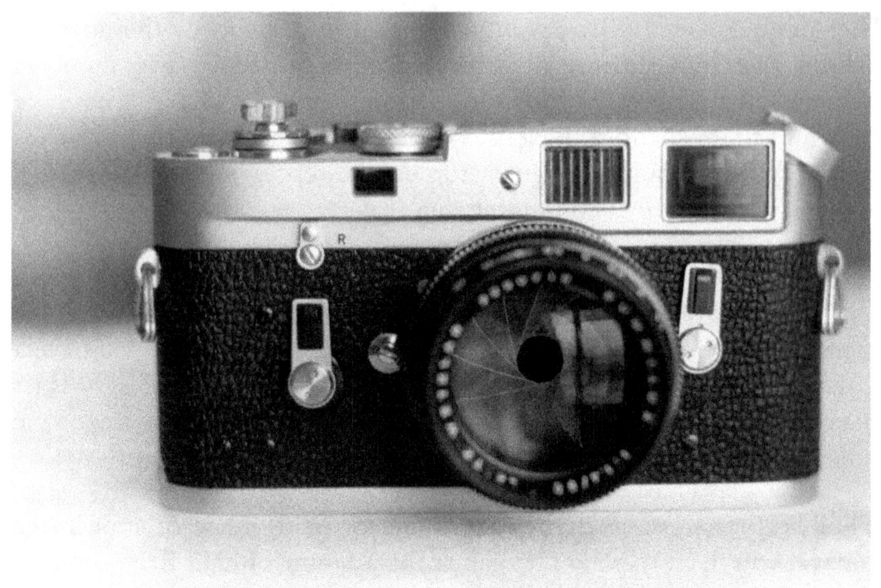

Shutter Speed

How it Works

The shutter speed is the third way to adjust your lighting settings on the camera. This controls how fast the mirror flips up and snaps back. The result is that light is only let in for the amount of time that the mirror is lifted up. The longer that the light is let in for, the brighter the image will turn out to be, and the quicker the shutter speed, the less light will be let in.

This setting must always be used combined with the aperture. The effect that you want on the image must also be taken into consideration, as well as the equipment that you have. If you want to capture motion blur in an image of a flowing river, you will set a low shutter speed and a high aperture, and you will need a tripod. While you want the water to blur slightly, you also want the rest of your image to be sharp, and the only way to keep it sharp when you are using such low shutter speeds is to have it stabilized on something such as a tripod.

Shutter speed is measured in seconds and in fractions of seconds. The slow shutter speeds would be 5" or 2", which indicates five seconds or two seconds. The fast shutter speeds are shown as 1/500 or 1/1000, which is a five-hundredth of a second or a one-thousandth of a second.

The faster shutter speeds freeze motion in the image. So if you want to capture moving objects as if they were standing still, you would use fast shutter speeds. This does let in a small amount of light, so you may have to widen your aperture or raise up your ISO to expose your image correctly.

Best Used For

Shutter speed is best used to freeze or add motion to your images. If you want an end result that shows the viewer that there was some movement in your image, then a slight bit of motion blur is great and can be achieved by using slower shutter speeds. This is great for creating aesthetically pleasing visuals of moving water or people walking in busy streets. It can be used in landscape photography, star trails, and other long exposure photography.

Other images will require you to freeze everything in the image, including objects which are moving. This time you will want to use fast shutter speeds in order to capture the scene as a frozen moment. You would most likely use fast shutter speeds in wildlife photography when you are trying to capture fast-moving animals—also, in sports photography, wedding photography, and other instances where you need extremely sharp images that are devoid of any unwanted blur.

Camera Exposure Modes

DSLR cameras offer standard exposure modes, in addition to the fully automatic setting on the camera. It is helpful if you are stuck and need to get decent images quickly, but is not advised if you want to have full control over your image settings. The best way to use exposure is to manually set each setting yourself in order to create the desired effects for your images. Despite needing to understand the craft and manipulate settings yourself, the camera does offer a few exposure settings to help you along the way. If you understand how each exposure setting works, it can be very helpful to use the preset settings in certain situations, especially when you need to shoot in places where the light source is constantly changing.

Aperture Priority (AV or A)

This setting is used when you want to have a specific aperture setting. You set your own ISO and aperture, which will remain fixed for as long as you use this setting or change them yourself. The camera will then automatically adjust the shutter speed in order to get the exposure value correctly in the center for a well-exposed image.

Shutter Priority (TV or S)

This one works the same as the above setting except that you set the ISO and shutter speed while the camera automatically adjusts the aperture value according to the light that is available.

Bulb (B)

The bulb setting is used when you want to have a shutter speed that is longer than 30 seconds. You choose the ISO and aperture values before using a remote shutter release to take the image. Pressing the button once will open the shutter, and it will only close once the button is pressed again. A remote shutter release is vital here as any sort of movement that the camera makes will show up as camera shake on the image.

Manual

If you are ready to become professional, then this is the setting for you. Using manual gives you full control of all three exposure settings, and they will only change when you adjust them yourself. This setting ensures that you will always have your images exposed just how you would like them to be, as long as you understand the fundamentals of each exposure setting, as explained above.

Exposure Summed Up

You can now see how all three settings need to work together in order to correctly light up your image. The key is to first determine what effect you would like to have on your image. Then change the setting that creates that effect. Finally, balance the other settings so that you correctly expose your image. Some effects which you may want will have a specific aperture and shutter speed setting to achieve it, leaving you to adjust your ISO if the exposure does not line up correctly. Exposure is not something that needs to be perfectly accurate every time. While the EV on the light meter is a helpful tool, it should not stop your creativity in any way. Use the meter as a guide but be sure to change it up, as some images work well with a darker tone with certain areas being left underexposed, this adds mystery and intrigue to the image, and other images may need a very bright feel. The light meter might be slightly off at times, too, if the focus was not on the correct subject when it measured the light. Be sure to check your images as you take them to ensure that your exposure is correct.

Shooting Prompt: Open up your aperture to the widest and take a photograph of a line of objects. Slowly start closing the aperture (adjusting shutter speed as you go) until it is at its narrowest. See how the depth of field is affected.

Composition

The focus point or points of an image are important to catch the eye of the viewer and take them on a journey into the image. A well-composed image will direct the viewer's eyes to look at the different objects in a very specific order, telling the story of an image as the photographer wants it to be told. The image must first grab your attention with a hook and lead you through all the elements while offering a satisfying conclusion.

If the image is too cluttered, and there are no obvious lines for the eye to follow, the viewer will get distracted and turn away from the image. When people view images, they do not want to work to understand what the image is saying, and they don't want to have to look for the main point of interest of the photograph. They want it to be an effortless task where their eyes naturally scan over the image, knowing exactly what the point of the photograph is.

What is Composition?

The composition is understood as the layout of the image itself. It is where and how the objects within the image are arranged and placed to create aesthetically pleasing scenes. It is the arrangement of the visual elements which are found within the photograph. The placement of the image details needs to offer the viewer the chance to interpret the feelings and expressions of the subject matter.

While achieving the correct exposure is important in producing a well-lit image, the composition is important to make a statement with that image and make it memorable. A good composition will leave the viewer feeling satisfied that they understand the essence of the image even if they don't really understand the image itself. This is because the image will feel complete, as if the story has a well-composed ending.

Putting a lot of thought into the composition and how you set-up your scene before taking your photograph will set you apart from amateur photographers.

The image must have a beginning. The viewer's eye should immediately be pulled towards the main focus of the image, then shown the context of the image, and lastly, shown where the image has ended or where the eye should leave the page. You can manipulate your scenes to create great compositions by the angle from which you shoot the image, the framing of the shot, what is left out or included in the image, and the placement of each element within the image. The colors and contrast in your image will also lend to the composition that you end up creating.

Types of Composition

The composition of your image can follow many different guidelines. Below are some examples of what you need to take into consideration when executing your shot. These can be used together to create various compositions and results. While these are the rules, we know that rules can be broken when it comes to the creative industries. However, it is always important to know how to follow the rules in order to creatively break them.

Rule of Thirds

The rule of thirds is one of the easiest rules of composition, but it makes a world of difference to the end result of your images. To execute the rule of thirds, imagine that the image in your viewfinder is divided with two horizontal lines and two vertical lines, intersecting each other to create a grid of nine equally sized rectangles. The rule of thirds means that your main subject in the image must sit on one of those lines, and even more precisely, on one of the four intersection points. This means that the subject must not be directly in the center of your image, as this can lead to flat and boring image compositions. As with most rules, there are exceptions, and in some cases putting the subject dead center can be very powerful. This is especially true with compelling portraits.

Most DSLR cameras will have the option to view the grid in your viewfinder, which shows you the rule of thirds lines while you view your scene, this will make it easy when you need a guide to get you started with the rule of thirds. The image below shows the grid on the camera screen while the photographer is setting up the shot. The first point of focus is where the train tracks are thick on the right of the photograph, and the literal lines of the train tracks guide you through the image to the second point of focus, which is where the train tracks just begin to turn and disappear. This composition takes the viewer along the tracks and leaves them at the turn where they can continue their journey and imagine where the tracks would lead.

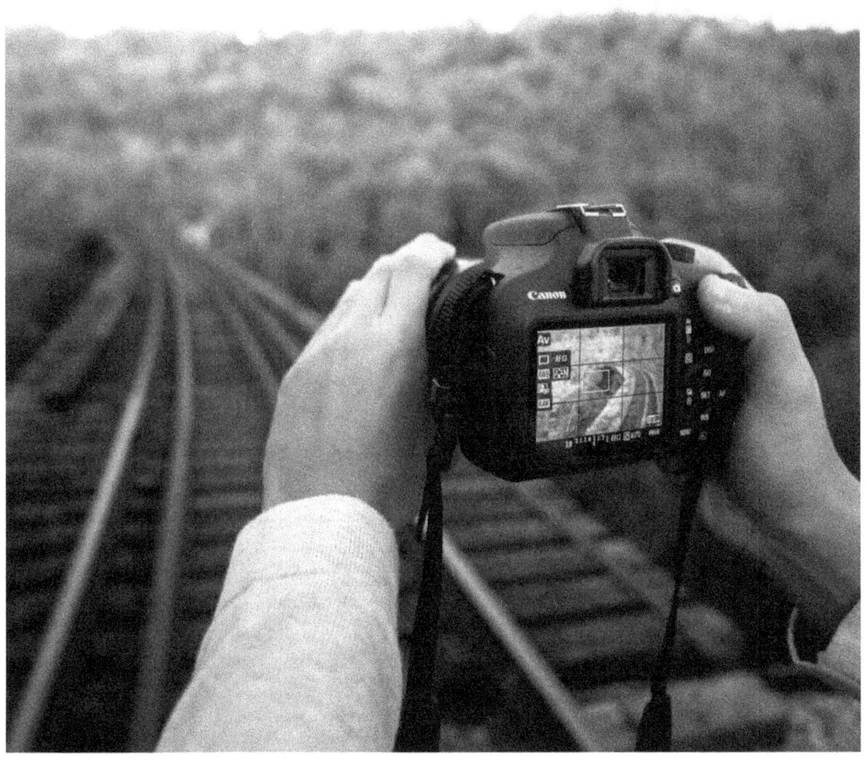

One of the most important times to remember this rule is when shooting a landscape that contains a horizon and shooting where there are other strong, straight lines. The key is to not let the horizon or line sit in the middle of the image, as this results in the line cutting the image in half and leaving the eye confused as to where to look. The eyes end up viewing the image as two separate images instead of one whole complete one. The exception is if you desire this effect if you are trying to show a comparison where you are essentially showing two images and how they contrast each other.

When a split is not the intention, you should let your horizon sit on one of the grid lines, depending on where you want your focus. If your sky has compelling details, then you will place the horizon on the bottom line to emphasize the sky. The reverse is true, too, when you would like the foreground to stand out—you would place the horizon on the top line.

Framing

Framing is the act of creating a frame around your main subject in your image. This can be completely natural or manmade framing. To frame a subject, you need to set your subject up in a way that allows the surrounding objects to create a frame around it. This can be done by using doorways, bridges, branches hanging from trees, or even buildings. To manipulate the frames, you will need to be strategic in where you place your subject as well as what angle you set the shot up from.

Using a frame in your composition will help direct the viewer to the main point of interest while removing any unwanted details or objects. You can always keep your eye out for different types of frames in the areas where you are shooting. When using a frame in your image, make sure to include the entire frame so that it does not get cut off at the edge of the image.

It is up to you on whether you would like the frame to be as sharp as your subject, by using a narrow aperture of f11 and upwards. Alternatively, to blur out the frame and focus on your subject, using a wide aperture. Either one can be used to create compelling photographs.

When you do not have a frame within your image, the edges of your image become the imagined frame, and it is important to keep this in mind when you are capturing moving objects. When your subject is showing movement (even if they are sharply in focus) or facing a certain way, it is important for you to place them as a lead into the image.

A good way to understand this is if you are shooting an actual person in a walking movement, you should place them so that they appear to be walking into the frame, rather than walking out of the frame. . The viewer will want to follow the subject. If they are close to the edge, the viewer will follow them straight into the image to determine what they are walking towards. If the subject is placed walking out of the image, then the eye will follow straight off the image without seeing what else is in the frame, since the viewer is curious to see what the subject is moving towards. It is important to allow the viewers to journey with the subject into the photograph.

Context

The subject of your image is not the only thing that is important. The subject needs some sort of context, even if that context is nothing. The foreground and the background surrounding your subject is just as important as the subject. Having certain objects visible can help to add context to your subject, telling the story of why your subject is there, and why you have placed your subject in that way. It tells the message of the image. If the objects surrounding your image do not add context or relevance, they may be unnecessary, and you would be better off to remove them by switching angles or scenes. The viewer would prefer not to have a cluttered scene that isn't adding anything to the image because it becomes distracting, and the eye will get tired and look away. If there is nothing but the subject in the image, then this adds enough context as the subject will be strong enough to carry the story. This is if you manage to compose the subject correctly to provide its own context.

The foreground context is important as it is often the entry point into the photograph. A well-placed foreground object can pull the viewer in and direct them where to go next., and the background of the image is just as important to complete the image. Having context helps to pull the image together, resulting in a well-packaged image ready to please the eyes of the viewers.

Weight and Balance

Weighting in terms of the composition refers to the various visual weights, which are evident in the image. The weighting is determined by how much visual impact the objects or colors have, and having a well-balanced image leads to aesthetically pleasing results. To balance the weights, you must understand what a heavy and a light weight is in terms of objects in an image. Different factors, such as colors, people, the actual size of objects, and contrast can all affect the weighting of an image.

When you understand balance here, it is best not to think about the scales lining up. Instead, this type of balance is more suited to be understood by hierarchy. You want to make sure that your image has something strong to pull the viewer in, which should be a heavy element, followed by less prominent objects that accompany the main focus in a complementary fashion. This creates balance. You cannot have two heavy objects in an image competing for attention, and in the same breath, you cannot have only light objects in an image. In both instances, the eye will have no clear path of where to look and will become restless while trying to find a point to land on. Good images capture and hold people's attention. A cluttered or confusing image will not achieve this.

Symmetrical balance is when you have two equal weights balanced by the center of the image, creating formality in the composition of the image. This balance may not always work as it can feel too static and predictable.

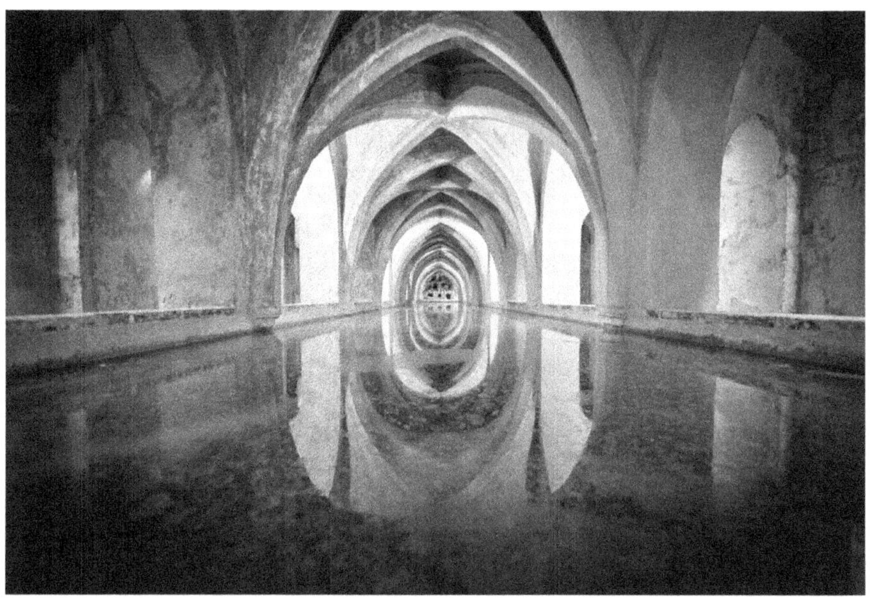

Asymmetrical balance is understood when there are unequal elements making up the image. Having one heavy object on one side with a few smaller objects on the other side can create a balanced image that is more diverse and interesting.

Color can also affect the weighting of an image. Bright and bold colors capture attention better than lighter colors. Having a strong color will draw the eye towards that object, so make sure that is where you want the focus on your image to be.

Mastering contrast is another way to balance an image. Images with low contrast appear flat and boring as opposed to an image with high contrast.

Lines & Eye Lines

Lines in images can create a good composition if they are placed correctly. These lines can be literal or implied. The eye will naturally follow these lines, so make sure that they are heading to where you want the attention to be. Eye lines also lead the viewer, as humans are curious beings and so the automatic response when seeing an image of a person will be to look where they are looking. So make sure that you are leading the viewer correctly with these lines.

Shooting Prompt: Rule of thirds. Go out and use the rule of thirds grid in your viewfinder or your imagination to place your main focus on one of the thirds lines.

Photographic Techniques

There are so many different techniques to learn when you are beginning photography, such as manipulating light and your subject matter in order to create aesthetically pleasing results. You can use light, create more light, or add blur to your images, and the list goes on and on. There is no way to teach all these techniques in a general book such as this, and the types of techniques that you need to learn will differ in the area of photography that you choose to dabble in. However, this book did promise to get you going on your creative journey, so here are two techniques to try out when starting your photographic mission. Panning is a fun trick to learn, but to truly master it is quite intense. Long exposure photography is another exciting technique to learn; this allows you to take those moody night-time shots or star trails. You will definitely need a tripod for this technique.

Panning

What is Panning?

Panning in photography is the act of portraying a moving object sharply while still giving the viewer context that it is, in fact, moving. This is where you may see a photograph of a car in sharp focus while the background around it is blurred out, showing that the car is moving. This is different from intentional motion blur where the moving object is blurred out while everything else is fairly sharp. When creating motion blur, you are often staying still while shooting a moving object; now, you will need to move with the object in order to successfully pan an image.

When panning, you want the moving object to be frozen and sharp while the rest of the image indicates the motion. This is because your moving object is your focus, and the background detail is not as important. The effect of panning is to give your image motion, and in most cases, it indicates speed. The object in your picture is seen as fast-moving since the surroundings are blurred out in a way that creates motion streaks. Panning is a great way to capture moving animals in wildlife photography or cars for car adverts or in action sports photography.

How to Pan an Image?

When creating a panning effect in photography, you need to follow the moving object with your camera to capture a sharp image with the background in motion. These are the steps that you can take to create this effect.

Firstly, you will need to set relatively low shutter speeds in order to create a blur effect. This speed will vary based on the speed of the subject and your camera's focal length. Slow-moving objects will use a shutter speed of around 1/15, while faster objects such as racing cars can go up to about 1/125. If you go too low with the shutter speed, you may get unwanted camera shake, so use a tripod that can swivel if you do go low. There is no way to give a set shutter speed, so to ensure you achieve your desired results, you will need to test and find the shutter speed best suited for your object. This is when it would be beneficial to use the Shutter priority setting in order to let the camera adjust the aperture to get the correct exposure while you focus on capturing that great shot.

Next, you will need to make sure that your stance is correct. You will need to plant your feet firmly in a comfortable stance as you must not move your feet while panning. Instead, you should follow your subject by swiveling your torso around. Be ready with your finger lightly placed on the shutter release and begin by aiming the camera where your subject will be coming from. Follow the subject with the camera while turning your torso. As the subject reaches the point where you want your photograph to be taken, press the shutter release. It is very important to continue to follow the subject further to complete the shot. Don't stop turning once you press the button, as this will result in your subject blurring.

It is important to remember that any movement on the actual subject could blur as well, such as a runner's legs. To correct this, you will need to adjust your shutter speed. So it is important to take some test shots with varying shutter speeds to create the effect which you are aiming to capture.

The tricky part in panning is to focus your image. Since the subject is not staying still in the area where you would like to shoot it, you will need to pre-set your focus. You can attempt to use your camera's autofocus setting, but this may not create sharp images as you hope, it will depend on how good your camera's focus is. To manually focus your image, you will need to choose the spot where you would like to capture the subject as it moves past, and focus your camera on that area. Once you have it in focus, leave the focus ring as is and move to get ready to start following your image. Even if it looks blurry at the beginning, the spot which you focused on should end up clear and in focus.

Practice is so important. Going out with your camera to practice with different shutter speeds and focusing is necessary to perfect this technique. You can practice on passing traffic if you have a safe enough area and this will help you learn which settings work best for your camera and your subject.

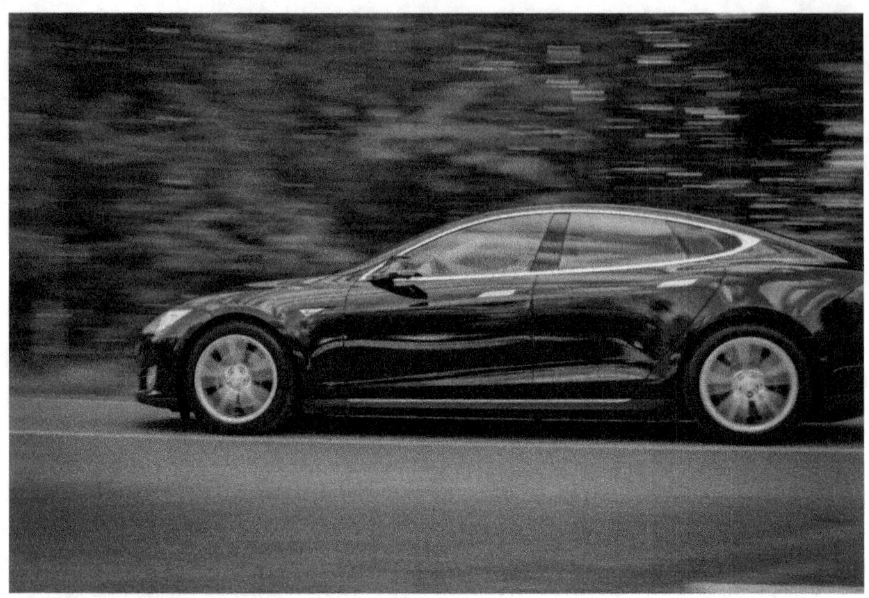

Long Exposure Photography

A very fun technique to learn is long exposure. It is pretty simple, but you do need a tripod to dabble in this type of photography. You have probably seen the landscapes with dazzling stars or night-time street photography. This is done by using your shutter speed to create long exposures.

What is Long Exposure?

Long-exposure is just as its name suggests. It is the opening up of the shutter for longer periods of time to let enough light in when it is relatively dark. This will allow you to light up those beautiful darker scenes and starry landscapes. The images you may have seen of lakes and rivers which have a glass-like texture and smoothness about them or the city scenes where the highways are filled with red and yellow streaks are examples of long-exposure photography. The purpose is to capture everything that happens while the shutter is open. Instead of freezing time, you are capturing a few seconds within a moment of time. Wherever there is movement, even slight movement, you can capture it with a long-exposure. Once you master this technique, you will definitely stand out from the regular photographers. When you are shooting long-exposures, it would help to also have a neutral density filter around to help balance the image so that too much light is not let in with the long shutter speeds. Even night time photography can become overexposed with the shutter speeds being so slow.

How Does It Work?

By simply opening up your shutter for a period of time usually longer than one second will allow your camera to pick up movement to create intriguing effects. Landscapes are a great place to start practicing long-exposure as there is a lot of movement in nature, so it shouldn't be too hard to find a good spot to set up. Make sure to check the weather to plan a time to go out. Clouds offer a more exciting scene than clear skies, while windy days can cause too much movement leading to blurry images that offer no focal point.

When using this technique, the image will not turn out as the scene looks in front of you. Using some imagination on how the image will look with the moving elements will help you when planning and framing your shot. In the daytime, be sure to avoid including the sun in the shot and the moon at nighttime, as these are strong light sources and will cause spots of overexposure in your image. Knowing exactly what you would like the end result to look like before you take the shot, allows you to plan ahead and map out the steps you need to take to achieve it.

Set up your tripod, and your shutter speed up by using manual, shutter priority mode, or bulb mode. Set the ISO to a reasonable f-stop for your lighting. The shutter will let in a lot of light, so the aperture should not be set too wide. You will need to test the shot here, even if you use a shorter time to judge how much light will be let in, this is the case for long-exposures which go for minutes and longer. If you are shooting 30 seconds, it is definitely worth testing at the right shutter speed.

Get ready to focus. It is important to focus the camera on your focus point and leave it on manual focus. You can either use manual focus from the start or autofocus on your main point, and while it is in focus, switch it to manual. This will prevent the camera from attempting to re-focus during the shot. Add on your filter after focusing and use a shutter remote release to avoid camera shake. Be sure to test that your focus is right too. It can be beneficial to cover your viewfinder when taking the shot to prevent any light leaking onto the sensor.

Be sure to use a remote shutter release and get shooting. Be careful not to bump the camera at all when it is shooting the scene as even small touches can cause distracting camera shake.

Shooting Prompt: Go out to the road and try panning with some cars driving past. Then take a long exposure of the stars at night.

Let's Get Creative

Now that you understand the basics of photography, it is time to flex your creative muscles. There are tons of sources to find inspiration and to get your creative juices ready to go out and capture some magic. Use this as a guide, but take it where you want to go, the most inspiring images come from photographers who are passionate about their subject material. Great photographers understand the subject and how it reacts to different lights and elements. If you shoot things that you do not find much inspiration in, your images will become stale and boring. You cannot fake passion. As technical as you are or how much you have mastered the camera, the emotion will not be there, and your images won't be taken to the next level or capture people's attention for very long.

This is the part to have some fun and bend the rules after successfully mastering them and see what you can create. Go your own way and create some shots that have never been done before. To get you started, here are some tips on where to find inspiration and where to begin playing around with your camera and its settings.

How to Get Inspired?

You can find inspiration in so many different places, and you should never limit yourself in ways to be creative. You can find inspiration sitting in public spaces, such as coffee shops, bus stations, or parks, or you can find inspiration looking out your window and watching the urban or nature scenes outside.

Technology gives you a platform to dive deeper into a world of creative inspiration; apps such as Instagram offer the perfect starting point to find inspiration. Use hashtags to find photographers who shoot the material you are interested in and see who they follow. Having an

Instagram feed filled with the types of images you want to capture is a continuous source of inspiration. Pinterest on the web is also a great place to pick up ideas and discover images that give you your creative spark. Pinterest is helpful because you can save mood boards for yourself which can help plan for shoots and get inspiration and ideas of what to add in the images and how to shoot them with tried and tested techniques.

Learn to Be Creative

It may be said over and over again, but it is so important to master the rules and then bend and break them to allow their twisted ways to create alluring scenes. Allow yourself to step out of the box and explore the mystical world that is out there. Even when you are shooting formal and structured shots, there is room to be unique. Something as serious as staff portraits for a large company can be crafted by what elements are included in the shot, and where the scene takes place. These can all be used to tell the viewer the nature of the work with only an image of the employees. Other areas of photography are naturally creative spaces, such as wedding photography, you want to capture the essence of the wedding, and this requires your creativity.

Learning to be creative is allowing yourself to let go of the rigid rules and seeing what happens when you color outside of the lines. It is best to practice these when you are not shooting for a client or a very special occasion, to master your creativity before showing it to the world.

Tricks Using the Camera

Motion Blur

Motion blur has been spoken of before, and it is when you purposefully shoot with a longer shutter speed to show the subject in motion. This adds movement to your image, and as a result, it can feel more interactive to the viewer as if they are in the scene since it is easier to imagine being there.

Try it out: People are an easy subject to catch in motion. It is easy to ask them to move in whichever way you would like them too. This is easier to set up your scenes than using natural elements that are unpredictable.

Emotion

Catch emotion in your shots to produce compelling images that catch the viewer's attention. Emotion can be literal using people's body language or facial expressions, or it can be implied. Moody shots can be used to create emotions as well as various colors.

Try it out: Ask the people in your photographs to try out some different emotions and see what the results are. Take up-close portraits with various facial expressions and see how the images make you feel, to help you learn how to use emotion to your advantage.

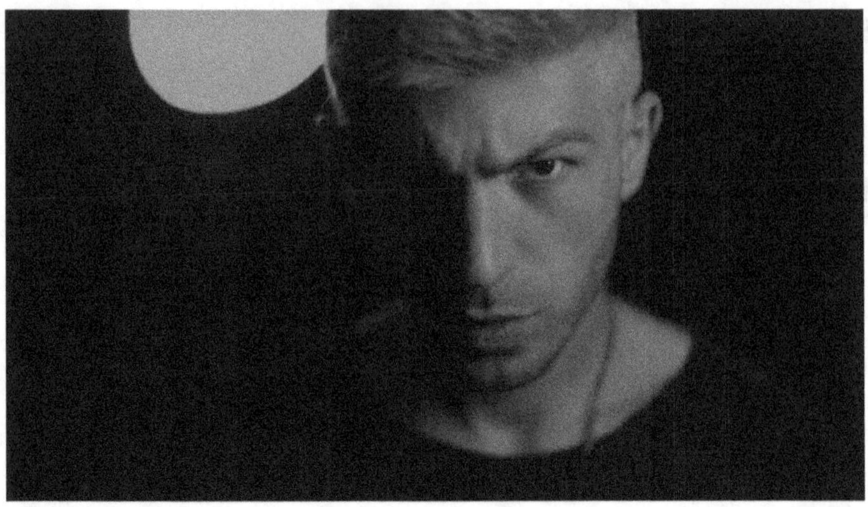

Angles

Using angles in your images can create a whole range of different effects. You may know that shooting from the bottom results in a powerful looking subject while shooting from the top gives off a weaker feeling. Go beyond this and try to use side angles, or exclude information from the scene to create a more intriguing effect.

Try it out: take a shot with your camera on the ground and see what effect it produces. Try shooting a subject upside down with your camera as close to the ground as possible, see what effects it creates, you may create an image which looks like your object is hanging in the air.

Perspective

Perspective is the spatial relationship of the objects in your photograph and how they appear larger or smaller than they actually are. Playing with perspective gives you the opportunity of creating a three-dimensional image; it grasps the viewer as they can almost step into the photo because there is space for them.

Try it out: Stand below a large building getting as close to it as possible while still keeping the whole building in the shot, make sure that you can see the top of it. Take the photo and see how small you feel when looking at it.

Shadow Play

Shadows are an intriguing addition to images; they create mystery and make the viewer want to find out more. They will look deeper into these images, if they are well-executed, to discover if there is anything more to the image. Photography may teach you to master the light, but to be great, you must also master the dark.

Try it out: Shoot an intriguing object against a wall in harsh light. Be sure to stand between the light source and your object and see what image it creates on the wall before moving up or down and to the side to see how the shadow transforms.

Bokeh

Bokeh is a favorite among photographers, as it is so easy to play around with and creates stunning and unique visuals. It is essentially shooting a blurry image of lights in order to create light 'bubbles', produced by how your lens captures the out-of-focus bits of light. Higher quality lenses will provide a more alluring bokeh feel. Bokeh is represented as circular-shaped colors of blur on your image, and you want to aim for soft and fuzzy bokeh as opposed to ones with sharp edges.

Try it out: Place an object in front of a colorful background. Use the aperture priority setting and open your aperture to the widest it can go (remember this is the lowest number). Focus on your foreground object and take the shot. Look at the background, and if your lens is good quality, it should produce soft, rounded bokeh.

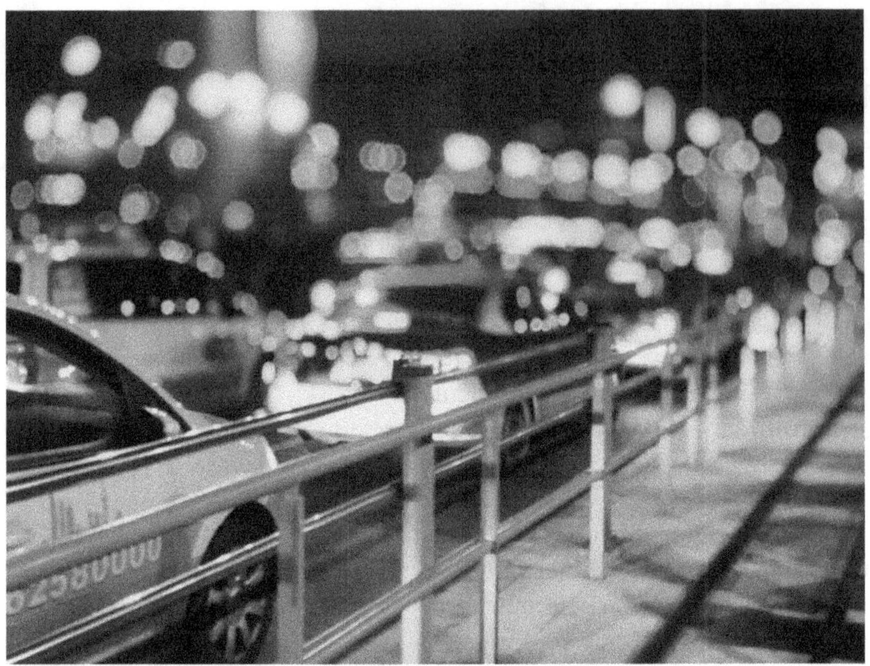

Light Painting

Once you have mastered long exposure, you can move on to playing with light more. Painting with light is a technique in which you use long shutter speeds and move a light source around in the image. The image will track the light source for as long as the shutter is open.

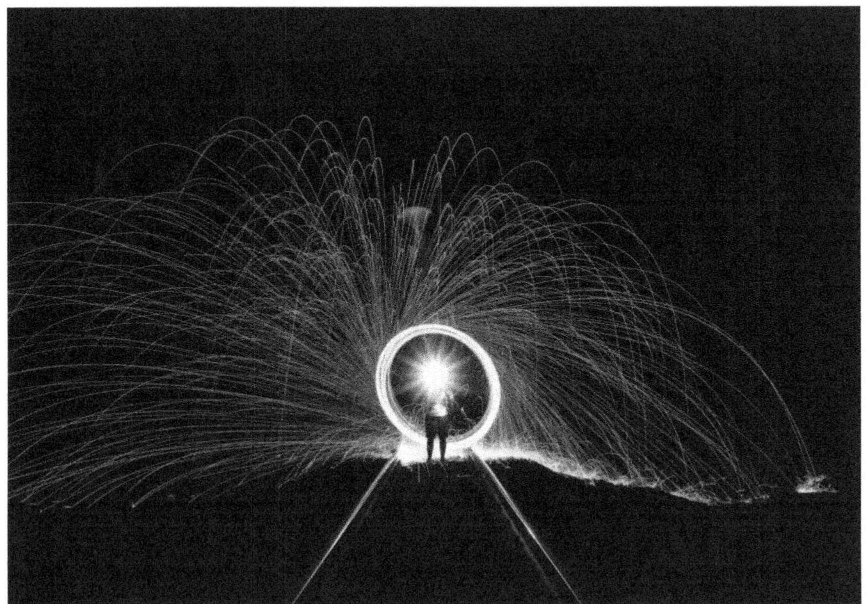

Try it out: In a dark room, place your camera on a tripod and use the bulb or shutter priority setting to open the shutter. Stand with a torch switched on and move the torch around in a shape against the wall that the camera is aimed at. Close the shutter and see what you have produced. Use different light sources in different ways to produce professional results.

Tricks Using Props

Create Confetti

You can get creative by adding texture to your images. Using white pieces of cut up paper and throwing them up in the air so that they fall around your subject when you take the shot, can create a snow-like effect. You can also use other colored paper to make other interesting effects. Be sure to use fast shutter speeds and play with the light and shadows around the subject.

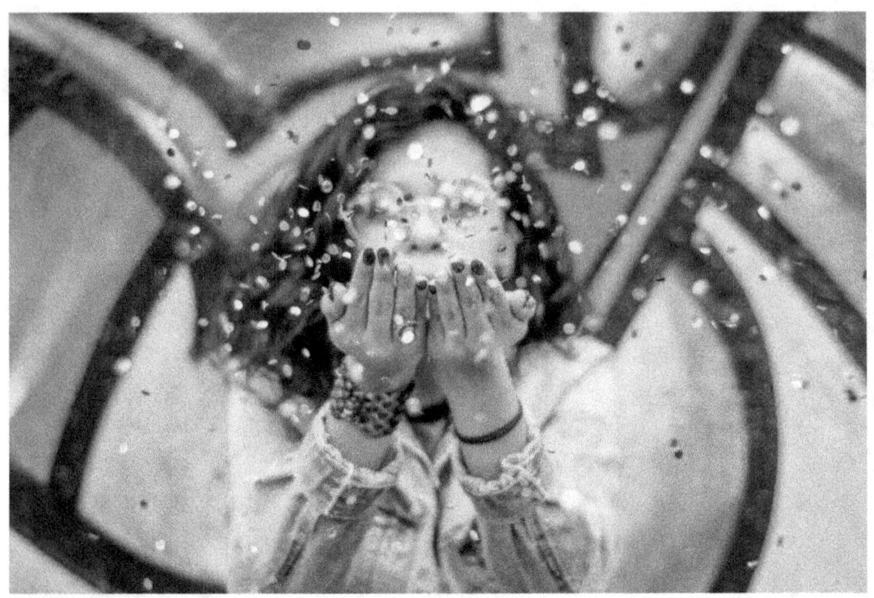

Color Smoke

This one may be a bit pricey, and not everyone will be able to access it. Although, if you can get your hands on some colored smoke canisters, go wild. Use a person to hold the smoke and create shapes around themselves with the smoke, or place it on the wet ground with some dark tones and low light and see what happens.

Reflections With Your Phone

Reflections are another favorite amongst photographers. You can find natural ones in bodies of water but get more creative by using your phone. Hold your phone screen side up, in front of your camera, and place your subject in front where it gives a reflection off the phone. The result is a mirror-like wonder. If you can exclude the edges of your phone by holding it very close to the camera, you will create an even better result.

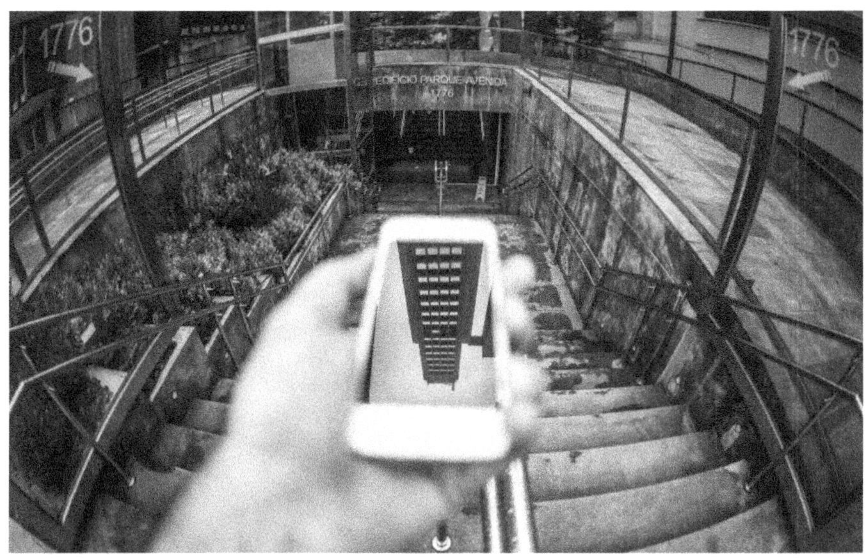

Use Fairy Lights

Fairy lights can be added to many scenes to make a more compelling image. Drape it around your object or frame your subject with the lights. Using different colored lights can make it even more interesting.

Create Rainbow Light

Rainbows are created by the light, which reflects off of water particles creating a colorful reflection. You can create this effect yourself by using glass prisms or even CDs along with sunlight or a torchlight. Use the chosen object to reflect the light onto your subject, and move it around to create different effects.

Camera to Desktop

Now that you have successfully created some magic with your skills and DSLR camera, it is time to share your images. To access your images and edit or share them with others, you need to first transfer them to your laptop. This is much easier than film, as there is no need to run down to the camera shop to have your photographs developed. Although, you will still need to head there if you want your photos to be printed on photographic paper. Having the freedom to sort out your own images and edit them even if you are a beginner at editing is a whole new world. You may have some images which just don't "pop" enough, and you can easily fix this with some quick post-shoot editing. Here are some tips when transferring your images.

When Should You Transfer Your Images

You should essentially transfer your images onto your computer in batches after you have completed each shooting session, to ensure that you always keep your memory card with abundant space. It is every photographer's nightmare to show up to a shoot with a full memory card of images that have not been copied over. Without any space, there is not much you can do, especially if you have images that can't be deleted, sitting on your memory card. It is also a good idea to have spare memory cards to swop out in instances where you find you have a full card. Be sure to check how much space you have available before heading out to those shoots.

How to Save Files

Transferring images to your computer is easy enough as most DSLR cameras appear as folders on your computer, and you can simply copy and paste the images to where you would like them to go. Be sure to save them in well-named folders so that you can have a good idea of where to find them. If you have shot in JPEG and RAW, you can split these into separate folders.

Formatting Your Memory Cards

When to Format

After each session of transferring your images to your computer, you should format your card once the images have been copied over successfully and the card is empty. Formatting is a way to wipe your card clean so that any data which may be left lingering is cleaned off, a type of reset for your card. Even if you have cut all your images from the card and they are on your desktop, you will still need to format the empty card to wipe it completely clean. This allows you to be sure that your card is completely empty, and it helps to keep the card running optimally going forward. Make sure you format as often as possible.

How to Format

Before you even think of formatting, make sure that you have saved all the data from the card that you need. Once you hit that format button, there's no going back, and that data will be lost forever. Now there are two ways in which you can format your card, either on your computer or on your camera. If you have your camera connected to your computer after transferring your files, you can do a quick format. Simply right-click on the memory card folder and hit format. Most computers will make sure you want to go ahead before commencing to ensure that you have not forgotten to copy anything you need. Allow the format to complete fully before removing the camera from your computer.

The other way is on the camera itself. When the memory card is inserted in the camera, and you have saved all your images to your computer, you can go into your settings and find the format option. Every camera will be different, so you will need to check the manual or go through your settings to find it. Allow the camera to take some time to format before switching it off.

Organizational Tips

Deleting

With digital photography, it is so easy to become trigger-happy and snap away thousands of shots in one session. A good practice is to try to become more thoughtful when taking images and set up properly before shooting. Although, it still can end up being a lot of images even when you are being mindful.

Delete some of your shots at the scene when looking through them on the camera's screen and delete any blurry images and test shots you have taken. If you are sure you won't use the image, then delete it right then and there. This will make it a lot easier to organize when you have them on your computer.

Once transferred to your computer, have another session where you go through and delete the ones which are definitely not working. If you are shooting in both formats, remember you will need to delete two files as they are saved separately. Be sure to check the file extension to know which is RAW and which is JPEG.

External Hard Drive

Since you will be taking a lot of images, and especially if you are saving RAW images, you will need storage space. Often computers don't have enough for photographers. External hard drives are very useful and can act as additional storage space as well as backup storage to prevent the loss of images in the event of any technical problems with your computer.

Folders

The folder structure you use in your photography is completely up to you. It depends on how you need to find and access your images, and a good practice is to include the date in the folders in order to find them easily or remember what is in the folder. Don't only include the date, though, also put the name of the shoot or your client's name. Even if you are just shooting for fun, start organizing from the beginning as the high volume of images can become messy. Breaking folders into months can also be helpful to show how much you did each month and to find them easily. Digital images from DSLR cameras can quickly start taking up a lot of space on your computer, especially if you are shooting in RAW as these files are larger than JPEG, so be sure to organize well and again, delete all the unnecessary images to clear up space.

Post-Shoot Editing

Now that you have your images saved to your computer and have deleted the less appealing ones, it is time to decide if you want to do some editing on your images. You may have taken images that are slightly over or underexposed or picked up some unwanted distractions in your image and need to cut them out. You need to now decide if you would like to do some editing on your images and how serious you are about it.

Either you will get a free program allowing you to do minor edits to clean up your images, or you will look at buying professional editing software such as Adobe Photoshop or Lightroom.

How Important is Post-Shoot Editing?

Post-shoot editing is entirely up to the photographer. Some may want to keep their images as natural as possible and show their skill through their ability to take great photos using filters and other equipment, yet, most photographers use some form of editing software for touch-ups. You may not always get the lighting correct, and if the shoot is busy and rushed, you may not pick up on things that aren't suited for your photo and will need to correct it in post-shoot editing.

The Moral Dilemma of Editing

There have been times when people have deemed it to be cheating to edit your images as you are not depicting the true scene, and manipulation leads to an unreal scene. While this may be true with some editing where creatives use their creative abilities to produce unique works of art, in other cases, it is not necessarily true. Cameras are very well-equipped to capture what we see in front of us, but they are still not as good as our eyes. People want to look at images that take them to that scene and place them in the middle of the action, and if the image does not depict what they would see if they were there, then it may not be as captivating. When newly-weds receive their wedding photos, they want to be taken back to that special day and remember what it felt like to be there and experience all those moments. In these cases, touching up images is not distorting reality but making the image more real by manipulating it to how it looked and felt on the day. Editing is also a great way to add that emotion and feeling to your images that cannot always be captured using only the camera.

Editing Programs

Free Editing Programs

There are many free editing programs and software which can be used for beginners to do minimal touch-ups for digital photographs. If you would like to test out how editing works on images, this is one way to do it, but it is not a substitute for professional editing. Free software is a destructive editing tool, and they can cause your image quality to not be up to standards for professional printing.

If you want a quick edit for photos that will stay on a digital space, these programs can be beneficial for a quick solution. They still cannot replace professional editing software to do a good job, and most do not cater to images in RAW format. If you are wanting to play around before making a decision on buying editing software, then have a look around and test it, but you will find that the capabilities are extremely limited compared to paid programs.

VSCO, GIMP, and Snapseed are examples of free editing software that you can try out on your phone or computer. Although, if you are looking at editing photographs professionally and for clients, then it is best to move straight to the paid editing software.

Adobe Photoshop

Adobe Photoshop can be purchased through the Adobe platform on a subscription basis, and is one of the programs offered by the Adobe Suite used for editing and photo manipulation. While Adobe is not easy to use if you have not learned to edit, it offers a huge range of photo-editing capabilities. If you are shooting in RAW, you are able to open it up in Photoshop to conduct non-destructive editing; you will see this in a window that opens before going into the Photoshop window. This allows you to touch-up the image and saves it as if you had taken the shot like that, as it does not reduce the quality or break down the image. The capabilities include contrast, exposure, highlight, shadow, and saturation manipulation, as well as cropping capabilities. There are more options in this window too. Once you have fixed up the image, you can save it in a JPEG format or go on to edit it further in Photoshop. There are many things that Photoshop allows you to do with an image going further than the slight touch-ups. You can create surreal imagery or fantasy scenes if you would like. There is no quick way to sum up Photoshop, as it would need a whole book on its own to describe all that the program can do.

It is important to remember that there are limits to how much Photoshop can correct an image that was not taken correctly. If the image has been under or overexposed too much, Photoshop will not be able to find the lost information. When an image is captured and has completely white or black parts, it is unlikely that you will be able to correct these areas even if you are shooting in RAW. When editing, if you are trying to fix the exposure and the image starts turning gray it is most likely because the information cannot be found to show the details you are trying to salvage.

Suppose you want to add specialized effects and manipulate your images a great deal. In that case, Photoshop will be your obvious choice as the tools in Photoshop allow for a lot of manipulation. Even if you only know the basics of the program, you will still be able to make a big difference to your images. Although, if you are shooting things such as event images with a high volume of images needed to be mildly touched up, Lightroom is a better option.

Adobe Lightroom

Also featured in the Adobe Suite, Lightroom offers many of the same tools which Photoshop boasts, but it is limited compared to Photoshop. While batch-editing is available in Photoshop, it is not its primary focus, whereas, in Lightroom, it has a strong focus on batch editing, letting you add predetermined effects or "presets" on a whole group of images in one go. It also allows you to effortlessly click through the images and make small adjustments to each image. It offers most of the Photoshop adjustments such as exposure, saturation, cropping, and color altering, but it doesn't have the capacity for greater photo manipulation. Once you have made the changes in Lightroom, it allows for you to batch save the images and add a custom or general watermark on your images, this is suitable when you have hundreds of images to edit for clients. Although, if some images need more attention and editing, it may be better to take them into Photoshop to alter. Having both programs can be beneficial as it allows you the freedom to do more in your editing and save time while batch-editing the projects which don't require as much manipulation.

Common Edits

Learning to edit images is a continuous task. If you embark on the road to being a photographer and want to try extreme manipulation techniques, you will need to continuously learn and find new techniques and trends to stay relevant. It is a great task to do, and it will always be a fun journey if you find yourself dabbling in editing. While you can learn the basics from books or classes, a great way to learn how to edit is to follow videos on YouTube. There are many videos showing you step by step instructions on how to edit in the way in which you hope to edit your images, and having a visual component is helpful. However, here are a few of the more common edits that you will learn to explain the basics of editing and give you some inspiration and direction on where to start your editing journey.

Cropping

This is a very common technique in photo editing as many people accidentally include things in their images that they wish to cut out. Some of the time, it is impossible to cut any more of the scene out of the photograph if the lens cannot zoom in any further. In that case, cropping is a great tool to master and is fairly simple to use. Editing programs usually give you preset options of how you wish to crop your images, and these are shown in ratios, such as a 1:1 ratio as well as 4:5, 5:7, 2:3, 16:9, or unrestrained. These ratios are helpful as they allow you to crop an image to a specified size, and they indicate what the width should be in relation to the height, for instance, the 1:1 ratio is squared. When you use this ratio when cropping, it will keep the crop box as a square, and if you adjust it to crop more or less of the image, it will still stay as a square. The unrestrained option allows you to crop without a preset ratio, which means that you can cut off more of the width than the height or vice versa.

Be careful when cropping an image as you do not want to crop it too small or take out any details that are important to the overall composition of the image. You can easily take images without focusing on what is in the background as you know that you will be able to crop those out, but this is not good practice as you should be paying careful attention to detail when it comes to what you include or don't include in your image when shooting.

The crop is useful when you need to change the size of the image to a specific ratio for projects or if you have small pieces on the edges of your image which need to be cleaned up such as part of a lamp post or a person who walked into your shot at the wrong time. Be aware of how your crop will change the ratio. If you are using an unrestrained crop, you may not get the usual image ratio of images. This means that when you have the image printed, it may not fit into normal frames.

Spot Touch

Spot touch is another fairly easy tool to use in photo editing. This tool lets you clear up any blemishes that may have been included in your image. The most popular use of this is to remove pimples or unwanted marks on people's faces and bodies. It can also be used to remove birds from the sky or rubbish from the ground. If these blemishes are more in the center of your images and not on the edges it means that a simple crop cannot remove them without taking out important information, and if it is on a subject's body, it is even harder to remove. The spot touch tool is also available on some free editing programs, although these can easily create blurry spots on the image.

The spot tool can work in a few different ways. You can use a spot tool that blurs the unwanted area out to blend in with the rest of the area around the unwanted spot. This tool does this by using the information around the spot to guess what should be in the area you want to alter. This can grab information that is a different color to the area that you are changing and make it obvious that something has been manipulated. This is why doing it manually yourself on proper editing software is better than a quick fix. You can carefully clean up the area yourself. Another good option is the clone tool. This allows you to select the area you want to replace with a copy of another area on the image. This is a good option if you are fixing something in the water that is filled with ripples or movement, as the copy will make it look more natural.

Red-eye Removal

When taking photos of humans and animals, you can often get an unwanted red-eye effect, especially if the flash has been used incorrectly. This is often seen in point and shoot cameras where the built-in flash is too close to the lens. These red-eyes can be horrible, but since it usually affects the black pupil part of the eye, it is not too hard to fix. Some free-editing software can fix this up easily, or you can do it yourself. You can use the above spot healing tool or the red-eye tool in paid software programs.

Exposure

Exposure is one of the biggest edits needed to be done by photographers. Since the camera's light meter may not always be entirely accurate, it is sometimes necessary to adjust this slightly in post-shoot editing. Again it cannot be fixed if it is too far over or underexposed and will not lead to a natural-looking image. The adjustment tool works by lightening or darkening the image. Adjusting this on a RAW formatted image is the least destructive but can be done fairly easily on a JPEG formatted image too. This tool is essentially a slide which is sitting at 0 in its natural position. You can slide it to go over 0 or under 0 depending on which way you would like to adjust your exposure.

White Balance

The camera has a white balance meter, which is related to the warming and cooling effects that light has on images. In cloudy environments, the image can turn out with a slight blue tint while other images can come out with an orange tint. This makes your images look unnatural as those tints are not picked up by the human eye. You can set your camera to various settings to program it to lessen the tint. The camera can sometimes misjudge this and create an undesired color tint on your images. You can correct this in post-shoot editing by carefully adding in the opposite tint: adding more blue for the images which came out too orange and vice versa.

Sharpening

Sharpening is an important tool to use, especially if you are shooting in RAW format. When you use a JPEG format, the camera automatically sharpens the image to make it as clear as possible. Your image can only be sharpened as well as you focus your lens on the scene. This means that sharpening cannot fix a blurry image. This is to perfect those pixels slightly more after the image has been taken. When shooting in RAW, the camera does not take this step to allow you to conduct non-destructive editing. This means that if you are editing RAW images, you should use the sharpening option when you are finished editing your image, right before you save it.

Conclusion

This book has surely given you all of the tools to go out and succeed in your photographic endeavors. Learn the rules set out in this book well. Go and master them until they become second nature to you, and then you are free to bend and break them to create unique images. Photography is ever-changing and evolving, and there is constantly new equipment coming out. So when it comes to lenses and camera bodies, it is best to research before making any purchases when it comes to equipment. Know what you want before going in as you need to choose the right equipment suited for you.

The rules of photography don't change. The basics are there to get you started, and they are vital in taking good images. Learn and understand them well. Try them until you are bored with them so that they become second nature to you. This will help you get creative and step out of the box to create photography that is unique to your style. Even if you are only doing it as a hobby or for family gatherings, you can make those memories special by capturing them correctly.

Once you master the basics, go wild. There are so many new things to try with photography, and the creative ideas here can get you started. Take them further and keep adapting to the times. Keep up with the trends and what the latest photographers are doing to stay relevant. Then, go back in time and try out some old film techniques with your digital camera to see what you can create. Bring back old trends or expand on them. You can never be too creative.

Photography is a lovely discipline to know and understand, and it will allow you to capture great shots no matter what medium you are using. You will see your phone photography improve when you don't have your camera on hand, and you'll be able to take professional photos with the ever-evolving phone cameras as well.

All-in-all, photography is adaptable to the person taking the photographs. You need to take these tips and teachings and make it your own. Put your own emotion and style into your images, and you will become a unique photographer. Everyone behind a camera has their own way that they like to do things, so find your own. These techniques are the key to get you started. But you must take it further. Never stop learning and finding new inspiration. Now go out and get shooting, you know what to do, and how to do it. Capture that light.

References

Bradford, A. (2019, July 10). Everything you need to know to decide if a DSLR is right for you. Digital Trends. https://www.digitaltrends.com/photography/what-is-a-dslr-camera/

Favre, L. (2018). Six Black DSLR Lenses. In Unsplash. https://unsplash.com/photos/zae9zxwLbrA

Hull, C. (2011). The Complete Guide To Film Photography: 94 Inspiring Tips. Expert Photography. https://expertphotography.com/the-complete-guide-to-film-photography-94-tips/

Ives, J. (2015, August 23). Camera Lens Filters Explained | Chris Bray Photography. Chrisbrayphotography.Com. https://chrisbrayphotography.com/tips/lens_filters.php

Kraakmo, S. (2018). Person Holding a Camera Filter. In Unsplash. https://unsplash.com/photos/uAzUg6_tMCo

Ma, J. (2017, September 27). The History of Film Photography and Emergence of Digital Photography. Sleeklens - Handmade Professional Lightroom Presets. https://sleeklens.com/the-history-of-film-and-emergence-of-digital-cameras/

McIntire, J. (2016, January 14). How to Use a Gray Card to Get More Accurate Exposures and Color. Digital Photography School. https://digital-photography-school.com/how-to-use-a-gray-card-to-get-more-accurate-exposures-and-color/

Mihai C, A. (2018). Mad. In Unsplash. https://unsplash.com/photos/RMMWgYdtaEc

Owens, J. (2016). Black DSLR Camera Kit. In Unsplash. https://unsplash.com/photos/EXf5DjXytZE

Perkins, J. (2017). Long Exposure with Light. In Unsplash. https://unsplash.com/photos/P2PtvuImLRg

Rhee, A. (2018). Black Film Camera. In Unsplash. https://unsplash.com/photos/IheZ3LITH44

Ruiz, H. (2019). A Colorful Portrait. In Unsplash. https://unsplash.com/photos/e2pVrE1PYzs

Skipworth, H. (2014, August 19). Timeline: The history of digital cameras. Digital Spy. https://www.digitalspy.com/tech/cameras/a591251/world-photography-day-2014-the-history-of-digital-cameras/

Souza, S. (2018). Person Holding White Android Phone. In *Unsplash*. https://unsplash.com/photos/75BU3mfstOA

The Editors of Encyclopedia Britannica. (2013). Camera obscura | photography. In Encyclopædia Britannica. https://www.britannica.com/technology/camera-obscura-photography

Valery, J. (2018). Black Sedan on Gray Concrete. In Unsplash. https://unsplash.com/photos/RQub4zZuOCs

Wong, W. (2017). Person holding black Canon DSLR. In Unsplash. https://unsplash.com/photos/heD4zkB_iFI

Woodford, C. (2018, September 29). How do digital cameras work? Explain That Stuff. https://www.explainthatstuff.com/digitalcameras.html

Ying, J. (2018). Selective Focus on Cars. In Unsplash. https://unsplash.com/photos/66O3juvwC6g

Zocca, S. (2018). Concrete Archway Photo. In Unsplash. https://unsplash.com/photos/c8XFzHLCB0c

www.ingramcontent.com/pod-product-compliance
Lightning Source LLC
Chambersburg PA
CBHW050011070726
47598CB00014B/669